JOHN D. ROTH

Beliefs

Mennonite

Faith and Practice

Herald Press

Scottdale, Pennsylvania
Waterloo, Ontario

Library of Congress Cataloging-in-Publication Data
Roth, John D., 1960-
  Beliefs : Mennonite faith and practice / John D. Roth.
    p. cm.
  ISBN 0-8361-9270-2 (pbk.)
  1. Mennonites—Doctrines. I. Title.
  BX8121.3.R68 2004
  230'.97—dc22
                                        2004020519

BELIEFS
Copyright © 2005 by Herald Press, Scottdale, Pa. 15683
    Released simultaneously in Canada by Herald Press,
    Waterloo, Ont. N2L 6H7. All rights reserved
International Standard Book Number: 0-8361-9270-2
Library of Congress Catalog Card Number: 2004020519
Printed in the United States of America
Cover and book design by Beth Oberholtzer
Front cover photo by Wayne Gehman

10 09 08 07 06 05 10 9 8 7 6 5 4 3 2 1

To order or request information, please call
1-800-759-4447 (individuals); 1-800-245-7894 (trade).
Web site: www.heraldpress.com

Beliefs

*Dedicated to my daughters—
Sarah, Leah, Hannah and Mary—
with gratitude for the way in which their faith
and practice has enriched my life.*

Contents

Preface

Several years ago, while on a long flight to California, I fell into a conversation with a Japanese man assigned to the seat next to me. Initially, we chatted about the usual topics of weather, travel plans, and work. But it did not take long before our discussion moved into more serious terrain. As it turned out, the man was employed by a Japanese advertising agency that was trying to help Asian companies expand their share of American markets. Part of his assignment was to understand the inner logic of American culture, and he took his job quite seriously.

"I know from polls," he said at one point, "that Christianity is very important in American culture." But despite the fact that he had read several books about Christian history and theology, he still found it all rather mysterious. "Who was this person, Jesus?" he asked. "And why was it so important that he was killed in such a bloody way? Why do people still believe this? What does it actually mean to them?" His questions were sincere. Yet he clearly was bewildered. "Can you explain to me," he finally said, "just what it is that Christians believe?"

The question caught me off-guard. I found myself stammering a bit, and then feeling rather embarrassed for my incoherence. After all, I have been an active Christian for nearly all of my adult life. I teach at a church-related college. I lead a young adult Sunday school class in my congregation. And I am often asked to preach in local churches. I consider myself to have an active and reflective faith. I am not reluctant to talk about Christian topics. And yet his question suddenly seemed overwhelming.

How does one begin to describe what it means to be a Christian? Somewhere in my early upbringing I learned that "Christians don't dance, drink, smoke, chew, or date those who do." Was that the right angle to take? Should I try to explain who the Mennonites are, or would it be better to take a broader historical approach and explain Christian faith within the sweep of Judaism, the early church, Catholicism, and the Protestant Reformation? Perhaps I should start with the basics of Christian doctrine, beginning with the Trinity and then moving to creation, the fall, and the story of salvation. Or maybe I should just tell him that "I am a sinner saved by grace" and see where things would go from there.

My circumstance, of course, was made more difficult by our basic cultural differences. But at some level, the same basic challenge of communicating the essence of faith applies to Christians everywhere, regardless of the setting. All encounters between human beings, especially those that touch on our deepest convictions about the nature of reality, are cross-cultural in the sense that they require us to use language and logic to bridge the chasm of our different experiences and distinct identities.

For most of the history of the church, Christian assumptions were so deeply ingrained in public culture that the challenge of communicating or defending the faith to skeptics was never really an issue for the ordinary Christian. With the exception of scattered Jewish communities, virtually everyone within the borders of the Holy Roman Empire throughout the Middle Ages was a Christian—or at least they had been baptized as such at birth. Even though people did not always live according to its teachings, the Catholic church claimed authority over all aspects of public and private life, including politics, culture, and economics.

The Reformation, however, shattered the religious unity of Christendom. Each party—Catholic, Lutheran, and Reformed alike—claimed to speak on behalf of Christianity, convinced that it was defending God's truth. And each side was prepared to defend those convictions with the sword. The prolonged, bloody religious wars that followed in the late sixteenth and seventeenth centuries left Christian Europe deeply fragmented and religious leaders uncertain about how to advance their theological arguments.

The Enlightenment of the eighteenth century seemed to offer a solution to this new dilemma of religious pluralism and violence. Since religious claims based on the flimsy authority of personal conviction and private revelation were bound to lead to endless disagreements, Enlightenment thinkers insisted that all religious assertions must be based on the foundation of reason. After all, reason was a characteristic of the human mind shared by everyone, regardless of culture, class, social status, or religious convictions. Any religious claims not provable by the principles of logic would need to be set aside as mere opinion or superstition.

The strengths of such an approach were obvious. Grounding faith in the universal foundation of reason seemed to provide a peaceful way of resolving religious disputes while also promoting the gospel. Those who are clever enough to pursue their argument in a rigorous fashion can advance the claims of the gospel by backing opponents into a corner, where they will eventually need to submit to logic of reason.

The problems with such an approach, however, are equally clear. For if reason is to have the final word in all matters of faith, then Christianity is reduced to a series of logical propositions and doctrinal formulations. Powerful arguments on behalf of faith may bring your conversation partner into a formal agreement, but they don't necessarily bring about a transformation of the heart.

Equally troubling, rational arguments for faith often do not translate in a convincing way outside of Western culture, where the authority of reason over every aspect of human life is not so readily acknowledged. My Japanese conversation partner, for example, was a bright, rational person, yet from his cultural context the claims of Buddhism seemed every bit as rational as my arguments for being a Christian.

In recent decades, Western culture has witnessed a backlash against the rationalism of the Enlightenment. Recognizing that all claims to truth are always limited by particular contexts of language, culture, and personal experience, a postmodern approach to religion is likely to reject all efforts to persuade others in religious matters. "You believe what you want to believe," the argument often goes, "and I'll believe what I want to believe." Trying to convince each other of the truth of our private religious convictions is not only likely to fail; it also can easily become coercive—if not in outright violent ways, than in more subtle forms of manipulation.

There is much that seems plausible in this reaction against the confident claims of the Enlightenment. After all, anyone who has been in a cross-cultural setting will quickly recognize how many of our convictions about reality turn out to be merely the prejudices of our particular culture and upbringing. If things like musical taste, attitudes toward children, and perceptions of time reflect our cultural context, then why wouldn't religious preferences also be a product of the influences of our environment?

But this approach too, however compelling it may seem at first, has also proved to be unsatisfactory for most Christians. Ultimately, truth claims—those basic beliefs about the nature of reality itself and what it means to be a human being—are inescapable. After all, even the postmodern insistence that we are all products of our environment is an assertion about the "truth of the matter" that is just as unprovable as the claim that Jesus was the Son of God. At an even deeper level, arguing that religious beliefs are merely an accident of culture ultimately reduces faith to the level of a consumer choice or the accident of personal taste: you drink Pepsi, I drink Coke. Yet Christians understand faith to be anchored in a Truth that is much bigger than my personal whim, and much deeper than the accident of my birth or the idiosyncrasies of my culture.

So what are we left with? Is there *anything* about faith that can be communicated authentically to the people we encounter? If so, what does that faith look like? And how are those convictions best expressed?

This short book is an effort to respond positively to this challenge of summarizing Christian faith and practice from the perspective of a believer. Even though it is written primarily as a brief description of Mennonite faith and practice, at a deeper level it is also intended as a response to the questions posed by my Japanese friend about what Christians in general believe. "Always be prepared," we read in 1 Peter, "to give an answer to everyone who asks you to give the reason for the hope that you have" (3:15). This is one effort to do just that: to give a simple account of the Christian convictions that have sustained the Mennonite church for nearly five hundred years.

Chapters 1 and 2 focus on beliefs and doctrines that Mennonites hold in common with the broader Christian church. Even though some people—Catholic and Protestant alike—have historically regarded the Anabaptist-Mennonite tradition as a serious threat to society, the foundations of Mennonite theology are deeply rooted in the Christian tradition. Mennonites are, first and foremost, Christians who believe in the Bible, the Trinity, salvation in Jesus Christ, and a host of other doctrines that most Christians would regard as uncontroversial. At the same time, however, Mennonites generally approach theological discussions from a distinctively "incarnational" perspective—that is, doctrines of the church become most meaningful for Mennonites only as they are actually embodied, or lived out, in daily life.

Chapters 3–11 focus on four interrelated themes in the Mennonite tradition: biblical interpretation, baptism, discipleship, and the church. Each theme follows a similar structure. After summarizing the distinctive Mennonite understanding of each concept, a subsequent chapter highlights several points of concern or disagreement that other Christians have raised in response to the Mennonite perspective. My intention here is neither to summarize every nuance of theological disagreement nor to oversimplify the perspectives of other Christian groups. But Mennonite theological understandings are best understood as an ongoing conversation within the broader Christian tradition, in which convictions often become clearest when they enter into dialogue with alternative perspectives.

In a similar way, each of these chapters also identifies a series of additional questions that remain unresolved within contemporary Mennonite congregations. The point here is not to air dirty laundry or to celebrate diversity for its own sake. Rather, Christian faith in the Anabaptist-Mennonite tradition is understood to be a dynamic process, always engaged in the task of discerning God's will in conversation with other believers as we face new challenges and circumstances. It is my hope that identifying these points of difference will encourage healthy conversation both in ecumenical contexts and within local Mennonite congregations.

If, as the book suggests throughout, Mennonite faith is essentially incarnational in nature, it is fair to ask the larger question of how contemporary Mennonites discern God's will in their life together. How do they live at the intersection between spirit and body, word and deed, faith and works? North American culture seems to offer modern Christians only two options. On one hand, we are pushed in the direction of moral relativism, where some believers are inclined to throw up their hands and give up on the possibility of identifying truth. On the other hand, we are tempted to retreat into the formulas of theological certainty, where Christians tenaciously assert truth without any hesitation or compromise. At its best, the Anabaptist-Mennonite tradition has called believers to reject both of these options and, instead, to live in a tension "between the times." Recognizing the persistent reality of our sinful natures, Mennonites nonetheless orient their lives around the teachings of Jesus, the empowering grace of the Holy Spirit, and the horizon of the coming kingdom of God. They seek to live *now* the kind of redeemed life that Christians anticipate everyone will live in the fullness of time. Together with Christians around the world, our daily prayer is that God's kingdom may come and his will be done "on earth as it is in heaven."

Sharp-eyed readers will have already noted some apparent inconsistency with my use of the terms Anabaptist and Mennonite. Strictly speaking, Anabaptim refers to a Christian reform movement that emerged in Europe in the sixteenth century. Inspired by the Reformation, the Anabaptists broke with the reformers by practicing believers baptism rather than infant baptism. Most Anabaptist groups also advocated a fairly literal application of Jesus's teachings that included a rejection of lethal violence and oath swearing, and promoted the practice of mutual aid along with a view of the church as a voluntary gathering of believers whose way of life would inevitably be in conflict with the unredeemed world.

By the end of the eighteenth century, descendants of the Anabaptists had differentiated themselves into three main groups. The Mennonites are named after Menno Simons, an influential Dutch leader in the middle of the sixteenth century. The Hutterites are named after Jakob Hutter, who helped establish the principle of community of goods. And the Amish are named after Jakob Ammann, who led a renewal movement in the late seventeenth century advocating stricter lines of separation between the church and the world. My focus in this book is primarily on the Mennonites. Sometimes, however, I use the term Anabaptist-Mennonite as a way of emphasizing the radical theological convictions that gave rise to the Mennonites. At other times I use Anabaptist as an umbrella term to describe the broad family of contemporary groups—Mennonites, Hutterites, Amish, and many other smaller spin-off groups—who claim a shared history in the Anabaptist movement of the sixteenth century.

Today, approximately 1.2 million Mennonites can be found scattered around the world, speaking dozens of different languages and reflecting a colorful mosaic of cultures and traditions. Though most of these groups would recognize and embrace the general themes highlighted in the text that follows, my point of reference is clearly Mennonites living in the United States, who comprise only about 25 percent of the worldwide Mennonite membership.

Some Qualifications

Trying to summarize the essence of a group's faith and practice is a risky enterprise. It is even riskier for a group that does not anchor its theological identity in a historical confession of faith (like the Augsburg Confession of the Lutheran church) or a clearly defined hierarchy of leaders (like the Catholic church). Although something by way of descriptive accuracy may have been sacrificed, I have tried to resist the temptation to qualify and nuance every point I make here about Mennonite beliefs. I trust that a few general acknowledgments regarding the limitations of this book might address the concerns of those hoping for more detail.

This summary of Mennonite faith and practice is not in any way an official statement by the denomination. Inevitably, the specific examples I use to illustrate my points will reflect the limits of my own experience and personal understanding. Nonetheless, the 1995 *Confession of Faith in a Mennonite Perspective* of the Mennonite Church USA and Canada serves as a background and touchstone for my summary. My intentions have been to reflect accurately the articles of faith stated in that document.

It should also be clear that my description of Christian beliefs from the perspective of the Anabaptist-Mennonite tradition is not intended to suggest that Jesus was a Mennonite or that the Anabaptist understanding of Christianity is flawless. Nor do I want to fall prey to the seductive temptation of comparing the best of Mennonite ideals with the worst of another group's practice.

Still, readers should know that I write as a convinced Mennonite, wanting to explain Anabaptist-Mennonite faith and practice in a compelling way. I want to be respectful and fair, but I do not pretend to be disinterested. After all, the timeless truth of Scripture and Christian faith is always expressed within the limitations of our particular context. In this sense, we are always bearing witness to the truth rather than claiming to have captured the truth.

One way of thinking about this challenge of trying to communicate a universal truth within our limited understanding is to consider the nature of light. All of us, of course, have seen light— we recognize it to be a fundamental part of our daily life without constantly asking ourselves whether or not light exists. Yet we never perceive light in an absolutely pure form. Sunlight is always refracted by the atmosphere. Artificial light is always conditioned by the lightbulb through which it shines. So in some sense the light that we see is always a step removed from the thing itself. The bulb is not the same thing as the light itself; indeed, it is always inferior to the light it projects.

In something of the same way, I hope this book will bear witness to the truth of the gospel, calling attention to the light of God. Ultimately, the purpose of these reflections is to draw each reader to a deeper understanding of the reality of Jesus Christ as the "Light of the World." At the same time, however, we can only see and experience that light through the lens of a particular language and tradition. It is my conviction that the Anabaptist-Mennonite understanding of faith is a faithful reflector of the light. I am convinced that it allows the message of Jesus to shine forth more brightly and clearly than other traditions. But I also recognize in making this claim that my description of Anabaptist-Mennonite beliefs is only a witness to the truth, not the truth itself.

An Invitation

Some readers may already be familiar with the Mennonite church, either as long-time members or as newcomers who are thinking about joining a Mennonite congregation. I hope that these reflections will ring true to what you have already experienced and encourage you to gain an even deeper understanding of the Christian way of life that you have already embraced. Perhaps this book will give you clearer language to express those beliefs that you have sensed to be true but have not always known how to put into words.

Some readers are not Mennonites and may have only a vague

understanding of who Mennonites are and what they believe. I hope that this book will enlarge your understanding of this small corner of the Christian community and possibly even correct some of your misperceptions. Although much of what follows will emphasize themes that distinguish Mennonites from other Christian groups, I hope that the many points of shared commitment with the broader Christian tradition also highlighted along the way will encourage more conversation between Mennonites and other Christians.

If, in the end, you disagree with the ideas presented here, you should know in advance that Mennonites are usually not inclined to make judgments on behalf of God regarding the status of your salvation. We take faith seriously; we rejoice in the truth but readily acknowledge that we do not possess it fully.

1

Christian Foundations

What Mennonites Believe

We believe in nothing other than what Christ taught and did, which the Apostles write about.
—HANS LANDIS (1613)

Ask any person randomly on the sidewalk what they know about the Mennonites and chances are good that you will hear an answer something like this:

"Mennonites—are they something like the Mormons?"

"Hmm . . . Mennonites? Nope, never heard of them."

"Sure, I know who the Mennonites are. They're the ones who wear black clothes and drive buggies, right?"

Mennonites are a relatively small Christian denomination, numbering only about 1.2 million members worldwide. Unlike the Amish—our more visible spiritual cousins known for their distinctive dress and a rejection of modern technology—Mennonites don't have a high public profile. Until recently, we have tended to live in rural settings. Our outreach programs have generally focused as much on relief and service as on winning souls. And we have been hesitant to promote our beliefs with aggressive campaigns or glossy media techniques.

Yet even though many people have only vague notions of who we are, the Mennonites have a long and distinctive history, firmly rooted in the Christian tradition. The origins of our church go back to the Reformation movement of the sixteenth century and, beyond that, to the early church of the apostles. Like all Christians, Mennonites read the Bible and believe in Jesus. We pray regularly, gather for congregational worship each Sunday, and try to make our faith visible in daily life. Mennonites share a great deal in common with believers across the spectrum of the Christian church.

At the same time, however, for nearly five centuries Mennonites have maintained a distinct identity, expressed in a variety of beliefs and practices that have set us apart from the Catholic church and most mainline Protestant groups. Today, in our culture of broad religious toleration, these differences may seem insignificant or of merely personal interest. But when the forerunners of the Mennonites—a group called the Anabaptists—first emerged in the 1520s, Catholics and Protestants alike considered their teachings so dangerous that they regarded the Anabaptists as criminals. Within a few decades of their beginnings, several thousand Anabaptists were executed. They were drowned, burned at the stake, or tortured to death on account of their beliefs, and many more thousands were imprisoned or exiled. In the centuries that followed, the Mennonite, Amish, and Hutterite descendants of these Anabaptists were rarely killed for their convictions. But they were often forced to live at the edges of respectable society and were generally regarded with suspicion or disdain.

Basic Beliefs

Contrary to what might be suggested by this history of persecution, Mennonites are first and foremost Christians, anchored in the deep tradition of the Christian church and committed to practice the teachings of Jesus as they encounter them in Scripture. In 1995, the Mennonite church in North America completed a lengthy process of formulating a confession of faith, a confession that merits closer study in its own right. Here I wish to highlight seven specific points affirmed in the confession that Mennonites hold in common with the broader Christian world. My intention is not to offer a systematic or complete summary of every doctrine that Mennonites share with the broader Christian tradition. And careful readers, especially those trained in the theological traditions of other denominations, may be quick to challenge the precise wordings of a given point or to insist that crucial nuances are missing. But since much of this book is focused on beliefs and practices that are *distinctive* to the Mennonite faith, the summary below may reassure readers who might share ancient suspicions that Mennonites are heretics. In a more positive sense, it also serves as a reminder that the foundation of the Mennonite church is rooted in a tradition shared by millions of other Christians. Even though we may not agree on how these convictions find expression, a focus on common beliefs does establish a framework for ongoing conversation and shared points of reference as we seek broader unity within the Christian church.

1. God. Mennonites, like all Christians, take as their starting point a confession of faith in God. Saying anything beyond this simple statement is always fraught with danger since descriptions of God inevitably strain the limits of our understanding. As soon as we try to define God with human language, we run the risk of reducing God to the limits of our own concepts and definitions. So we say, for example, that God existed before time itself or that God created the universe out of nothing. Sometimes we turn to the language of paradox (two assertions that seem contradictory, yet are simultaneously true) to describe God. For instance: God is both just (fair) and loving (forgiving); both righteous and patient; both all-powerful and all-merciful; unchanging, and yet responsive to our actions. Like other Christians, Mennonites are monotheists (we believe that there is only one God), yet we also affirm that God is made known to us in three persons, as the Father, Son, and Holy Spirit. At the very heart of our understanding of God is the simple conviction that the Creator of universe knows each one of us individually and that he loves us unconditionally.

2. Humans: Created in God's Image . . . Yet Sinful. Mennonites believe that God created human beings in his very "image and likeness." That is, humans were created for intimacy with God and bear within themselves something of God's very character and glory. And yet we also recognize that we human beings have consistently broken our relationship with God since the days of Adam and Eve. Something in our very nature seems to enslave us to patterns of behavior that turn us away from God, set us at odds with our fellow human beings, and make us want to live independent and self-centered lives. We allow ourselves to become trapped in the illusion that God is irrelevant to our world. This disruption of God's intention for humanity—what Christians call sin—is visible in human society as well as in individuals. Even social structures and policies meant for good purposes end up falling short of their intended design. Indeed, as Paul writes in Romans, "the whole creation has been groaning . . . [for liberation] from its bondage to decay" (Rom 8:21-22).

3. God Acts in History. Mennonites believe that despite our persistent tendency to selfishness, God did not give up on human beings. God does not permit the evil in creation and in ourselves to go unchecked, but patiently offers human beings the possibility of being restored to fellowship with God and to be reconciled with each other. The Old Testament recounts story after story of God's active intervention in human history, calling us back to the purpose for which we were created. Thus, following the flood God gave Noah the rainbow as a sign of his renewed love. God made a covenant with Abraham and Sarah, offering the promise of his blessing. "With mighty hand and outstretched arm" God led the children of Israel out of Egypt. God gave them the law and guided them into the Promised Land. And the prophets of the Old Testament spoke repeatedly of God's active concern for the weak and powerless—the widows, the foreigners, and orphans in the community. They also expressed hope in a Messiah who would restore humanity to fellowship with God.

The New Testament resumes this powerful litany of God's actions in history. With "signs and wonders" Jesus announced the coming of the kingdom of God. His teachings and miracles healed broken minds, bodies, and relationships. His resurrection proclaimed the power of life over death. The story of Pentecost and the missionary journeys of the apostles testified to the living presence of the Holy Spirit in the church that gathered in Christ's name. And, with all the Christians of the ages, we anticipate the culmination of human history in Christ's triumphant return. Mennonites believe in this powerful account of God working his purposes out in history, and we invite others to become a part of this great story.

4. Salvation in Jesus Christ, the Son of God. Along with the broader Christian tradition, Mennonites believe that at the heart of this grand story—the pivot around which the plotline revolves—is the person of Jesus Christ. God loved the world so much that he sent his Son, Jesus Christ. Through the life, death, and resurrection of Jesus, God offers salvation from sin and the possibility of being restored to full fellowship with God and with each other. Like descriptions about God, efforts to describe Jesus always stretch the capacity of our language. We believe, for example, that Jesus was conceived of the Holy Spirit, born of the virgin Mary, and was without sin. Yet he was also fully human, faced temptations, and experienced the same physical pain, loneliness, and sadness that we endure.

We believe that through Jesus we are saved by God's grace, not by our own merits. Yet the same Jesus who forgives our sins also calls us to "be perfect, therefore, as your heavenly Father is perfect" (Matt 5:48) and to "go now and leave your life of sin" (John 8:11). In his humiliating, unjust, and painful death on a cross, Jesus canceled our debt of sin. In his resurrection, he disarmed the powers of sin and evil. We receive God's salvation when we repent of sin and accept Jesus Christ as Savior and Lord. Mennonites are Christocentric—Christ-centered. As Paul writes, "For no one can lay any foundation other than the one already laid, which is Jesus Christ" (1 Cor 3:11).

5. The Church as the Body of Christ. Mennonites believe that Christ is most visible today in the community of God's people, the church. Throughout history, Christians have described the church in many different ways. Most would agree, however, that the church is not primarily a building or an institution or even a fixed set of rituals. Rather, we celebrate Christ's living presence through worship, prayer, and shared practices such as baptism and the Lord's Supper. These acts empower the church to continue Christ's ministry of mercy and peace that he demonstrated during his earthly life. The church is a spiritual, social, and economic reality, demonstrating in its life together and in its compassion for the world the justice, righteousness, love, and peace of the age to come. The world is still sinful, but Mennonites believe that members of the church are called to live now according to the principles of the future reign of God.

6. Holy Spirit. Mennonites also believe in the Holy Spirit. As with our descriptions of God and Jesus, language for the Spirit can easily become so abstract that it is almost meaningless or so precise that we end up reducing it to something we possess, like a butterfly pinned to a collector's frame. So we often speak of the Spirit in metaphors—as wind, or flame, or a dove. The Spirit of God created the world and inspired the prophets and writers of Scripture. By the power of the Holy Spirit, Jesus proclaimed the good news of God's reign, healed the sick, accepted death on the cross, and was raised from the dead.

The Spirit empowers the church. At Pentecost, God began to pour out the Spirit on all people and to gather the church from among many nations. By the gifts of the Spirit, Christians are called to carry out their particular ministries so that the church preaches, teaches, testifies, heals, loves, and suffers, following the example of Jesus. When we hear the good news of the love of God, it is the Spirit who calls people to repentance, convicts them of sin, and leads those who open themselves to accept the gift of salvation. The Holy Spirit comforts us in suffering, is present with us in times of persecution, and intercedes for us in our weakness.

7. The End of Time. Finally, Mennonites, like most other Christians, believe that the salvation we already experience is only a small taste—an appetizer—of the salvation yet to come at the end of time. Then Christ will fully defeat the powers of sin and death, and the redeemed will live in eternal communion with God. We believe in God's final victory at the end of our current struggle between good and evil. We believe in the resurrection of the dead, in his coming to judge the living and the dead, and in the appearance of a new heaven and a new earth where the people of God will reign with Christ in justice, righteousness, and peace.

Just as God raised Jesus from the dead, we believe that we also will be raised from the dead. The righteous will be raised to eternal life with God, and the unrighteous to hell and separation from God. We look forward to the coming of a new heaven and a new earth, and a new Jerusalem, where the people of God will no longer hunger, thirst, or cry. Instead, they will sing praises: "To him who sits on the throne and to the Lamb be praise and honor and glory and power, for ever and ever! . . . Amen!" (Rev 5:13-14).

A Summary: The Apostles' Creed

Some Christian groups remind themselves of these basic convictions by reciting the creeds of the church on a regular basis. Mennonites, by contrast, have not generally been inclined to express their faith in such carefully worded theological statements or to integrate the creeds formally into their regular worship time. Nonetheless, when questioned by other Christians about what they believed, Anabaptists of the sixteenth century frequently referred to the Apostles' Creed—a statement of faith that emerged very early in the history of the Christian church—as a summary of the key points of their faith.

Even though the Apostles' Creed, to a Mennonite ear, is strangely silent about the life and teachings of Christ—the crucial part of the gospel story that unfolds between "born of the Virgin Mary" and "suffered under Pontius Pilate"—Mennonites still affirm the statement as one important way of expressing their faith:

> I believe in God, the Father Almighty,
>> the Creator of heaven and earth,
>> and in Jesus Christ, God's only Son, our Lord:
> Who was conceived of the Holy Spirit,
>> born of the Virgin Mary,
>> suffered under Pontius Pilate,
>> was crucified, died, and was buried.
> He descended into hell.
> The third day He arose again from the dead.
> He ascended into heaven
>> and sits at the right hand of God the Father
>> Almighty;
>> thence He shall come to judge the living and
>> the dead.
> I believe in the Holy Spirit, the holy catholic church,
>> the communion of saints,
>> the forgiveness of sins,
>> the resurrection of the body,
>> and life everlasting.

So there it is in a nutshell! On virtually all of the major themes of the Christian theological tradition, Mennonites find themselves in alignment with the core beliefs of most other Christians. You may or may not be persuaded by the distinctively Mennonite theological convictions that comprise the bulk of this book. But readers who are concerned about whether the Mennonites might be a cult—or have confused Mennonites with Mormons, or wonder if Mennonites believe in God—should know that Mennonites are deeply rooted in the doctrines of the early church. We share the same biblical heritage, worship the same God, are empowered by the same Spirit, and seek to be faithful to the same Christ as the broader Christian church.

2

Christian Foundations

How Mennonites Believe

"No one can truly know Christ except one who follows him in life."

—HANS DENCK

A Mennonite Approach to Theology

I can still vividly remember one Sunday evening from my childhood, when our church rented a projector to show a film on Noah's ark. Those planning the service had advertised the event widely, hoping that the film's subject would pique the interest of the unchurched in our community. Once inside the church doors, the unconverted were confronted with archaeological evidence offering conclusive proof that the biblical story of Noah and the flood happened exactly as the Bible described it.

Though the full details of the film are no longer clear in my mind, I do recall the conflicted emotions I felt during and after the event. It was a relief to hear that stories from the Bible could be defended with empirical evidence. And I was pleased that the strangers in our church that evening would have to consider the hard logic of archaeological facts—facts that communicated the truth in terms that they took seriously. Yet at the same time I remember a vague disconcerting sense that there was something wrong with this blatant appeal to science to defend the trustworthiness of Scripture. If the truth of Scripture and the coherence of Christian faith ultimately had to be validated at the bar of reason, then the odd rituals of singing, testimony, and prayer, and indeed the language of faith itself, seemed unnecessary.

In a related way, Mennonites have traditionally been uneasy with descriptions of the Christian faith that are focused primarily on formal statements of doctrine. For Mennonites, doctrinal statements are a necessary but insufficient way of describing the essence of the Christian faith. On the one hand, doctrines are helpful and even essential for clarifying a baseline of convictions and for shaping a distinct identity. Since the Bible does not interpret itself and since circumstances continuously change, confessional statements such as the Apostles' Creed have helped to anchor the church within the context of a constantly changing environment.

On the other hand, Mennonites have also been wary about trying to distill the essence of their convictions into carefully worded logical language or highly detailed catechisms. After all, most of us don't stay awake at night wrestling with the concept of the Trinity. Nor are we accustomed to talking about our faith in the specialized, technical language favored by trained theologians. Furthermore, all of us know that there is often a wide gap between official church doctrine (the carefully formulated summaries of the principles of faith) and the actual thoughts, beliefs, experiences, and understandings of people in the pews. These are realities among all Christian denominations: lived faith is often messier than the tidy formulations of the theologians. Affirming a list of abstract beliefs may appeal to our sense of order and provide a clear language for expressing a mystery and majesty that sometimes defies our comprehension. But it does not adequately capture the essence of Christian faith.

The Christian doctrine of the incarnation is a helpful way of illustrating this concern. When Christians claim that Jesus is fully God ("Anyone who has seen me has seen the Father," Jesus says in

John 14:9), they are affirming the universal authority and tran-
scendent power of Jesus. Jesus, Christians believe, possesses all of
the characteristics that we use to describe God. Yet at the same
time, the incarnation reminds us that, in Christ, "the Word became
flesh" (John 1:14). God became tangible and visible to humans—
God became real—only by assuming the physical form and
substance of a human being. Ultimately, the doctrine of the incarnation preserves a deep mystery in the Christian tradition. It says
that Jesus was *both* fully God and fully human. If you take away
either side of this formulation, you destroy an essential aspect of
the nature of Jesus.

Mennonites think about doctrinal confessions in something of
the same way. On the one hand, creedal formulations are ephemeral
abstractions. They state deeply held convictions about our understanding of the truth, but in some sense they are merely words on
a page until they find concrete expression in Christian practice.
Doctrinal beliefs become real only to the extent that they are lived
out, or embodied, in the world of time and space in which we live.
Mennonites are therefore sensitive to the tendency of allowing
statements about faith to become a substitute for a lived faith. It is
not enough, we have said, to simply present our understandings of
faith as a series of propositional truths. The truth of these claims
becomes meaningful only as they are actually incarnated in the life of
the believer or in the collective work of the church.

This understanding has found expression in Mennonite theology in at least two distinct, though closely related, ways.

1. True Faith Always Finds Expression in Daily Life. In the first
place, for Mennonites, claims about God or definitions of faith are
not ends in themselves. Rather, they are ways of describing a living
relationship with God that ultimately must find expression in our
daily relations with other people. The greatest commandments,
Jesus taught, are to love God and to love our neighbor. Christian
doctrine can helpfully focus this commitment to love God and to
serve others, but it can never become a substitute for actually
carrying out these commandments.

From the very beginning of the movement in the sixteenth century, Anabaptists shared a deep suspicion of the so-called *Schriftgelehrten*—the university-trained scholars who, they claimed, artfully dodged the clear and simple teachings of Jesus by appealing to complex arguments and carefully crafted statements of doctrine. In other words, they confused theological discussions with lived faith. Repeatedly in court testimony and in formal disputations, one can hear the exasperated voices of the theologians trying to coax the Anabaptists out of a stubborn focus on applied faith into the arena of doctrinal debate—usually without succeeding.

Like our Anabaptist forebears, Mennonites today tend to emphasize the practical life of Christian discipleship more than debates about abstract points of doctrine. We are often clearer about the standards of how we should live (orthopraxis) than about what it is that we should believe (orthodoxy). Some writers have described this as *existential faith*. It is a faith that is understood only as it is actually lived. Others see this approach as a *pilgrim faith*, in which we are united more by a clear commitment to a common journey than by a highly detailed map that has each step of the itinerary carefully mapped out in advance.

At the heart of this position was a profound claim stated succinctly by the Anabaptist Hans Denck: "No one can truly know Christ except one who follows him in life." Knowledge of Christ is inseparable from a life of discipleship. Faith becomes faith as it is incarnated in daily practice.

2. True Faith Is Always Noncoercive. In a similar way, Mennonite hesitance about doctrinal statements reflects a deep commitment to an understanding of Christian faith that is rooted in nonviolence. To be sure, most people today do not think of confessions of faith as potential weapons. But from the Anabaptists' painful experience in the sixteenth century, Mennonites learned that claims to absolute certainty about faith—as expressed in carefully formulated systematic statements—could easily provide a rationale for condemning to hell all those who disagreed. Or, as often proved to be the case, the interrogator's faith could be used to justify the Anabaptists' execution as heretics.

Throughout history, Christians have faced the persistent tempta-tion of confusing the language we use to talk about God with the essence of Christian faith. This stubborn human tendency to turn doctrine into an idol—to confuse a human creation with the truth itself—can easily lead people to wield doctrinal claims as a weapon against minority or dissenting perspectives. Thus, anyone who does not line up with a certain formulation of Christian faith is not only wrong, but also a heretic and therefore worthy of punishment or death.

Mennonites, by contrast, understand Christ's invitation to love our enemies as central to the good news of the gospel. Just as God extended love to us while we were still sinners—"enemies of God," as Paul says in Romans (5:10)—so too, ought Christians to extend that same gracious love to others. This simple conviction, we believe, is at the very crux (cross) of the gospel: Christ, who held the power of God in his hands, voluntarily relinquished that power, became a servant, and suffered a humiliating death on the cross in order to demonstrate, through his resurrection, that love is ulti-mately more powerful than the forces of evil and death. For Mennonites, this basic conviction is the foundation for virtually all of their theological reflection.

Concretely, as we will see in more detail in later chapters, this means that Mennonites are committed to incarnating God's love in their daily life. But in a more subtle form, it means that the *method* of proclaiming the gospel has to be consistent with the noncoercive substance of the message that we are proclaiming. Thus, true Christian witness can never proceed as an argument designed to bully the listener into a corner with clever arguments or overpow-ering rhetoric. Instead, Christian witness always proceeds as an invitation. Rather than basing our testimony on "Four Spiritual Laws" or a verbal assent to a series of doctrinal claims, Mennonites are more inclined to allow the teachings of Jesus to speak for them-selves. Or they bear witness to the power of Christ's love and the transforming reality of the resurrection by the example of their daily life. In any case, the invitation is to a transformed way of life—not to a certain emotional state or set of intellectual propositions.

This commitment to frame their understandings of truth within a context of patience and humility has also had consequences for how Mennonites organize their church. Some Christian traditions (the Catholic and Episcopalian churches, for example) have a clear structure of authority that enables the church to speak with clarity and precision in matters of doctrine. When a controversial point of doctrine emerges, those within the church hierarchy with formal authority to instruct others in matters of faith consider the question carefully and then hand down the correct interpretation of Scripture. In the Catholic tradition, it is the pope who has the final word in matters of doctrine and belief. Even though lay people may grumble, or even choose to disregard the church's teaching, the lines of authority in matters of biblical interpretation are quite clear.

Not so among the Mennonites. Mennonites have generally assumed that the Bible is best interpreted in local settings—within congregations or regional conferences—rather than by a central teaching office or a hierarchy of bishops. To be sure, Mennonites do have ministers with seminary education, and the voices of some teachers in the church are widely respected. But Mennonites generally assume that biblical study and interpretation is appropriately the task of *all* members of the church, not only those in specially appointed positions. Although this can open the door to a diversity of perspectives, one clear strength of this approach is that it honors both the unique voice of each member and the collective wisdom of the whole community. For a Mennonite, commitment to Christian faith cannot be passive. Study, reflection, discernment, and action are expected from every member.

So Mennonites live in a kind of tension: the doctrines of the Christian tradition give us some necessary principles for interpreting Scripture and staying focused on the essential themes of Christian faith. But those doctrines are understood as human efforts to describe a mystery that always, necessarily, exceeds our grasp. Christian humility appropriately reminds each of us—as individuals and as groups—that we do not have absolute understanding of the ways of God. And yet, at the same time, a desire for unity in the body of Christ should compel us to seek out points of shared belief and practice, so that our conversations about differences can move in a direction that is constructive and loving, rather than merely defensive.

Unity Amid Diversity

For those outside the Mennonite tradition, this distinctive approach to belief will likely appear to be a weakness. "After all," you might be inclined to argue, "how can you know what you believe if you don't have it all down on paper somewhere?" or "Who's in charge? Doesn't someone have to have the final say?"

There is some truth in these concerns. In the absence of a clear hierarchy of leadership or absolutely fixed statements of doctrine, Mennonites have tended to proliferate into a colorful mosaic of subgroups who, from the outside at least, appear to have little in common with each other. After all, what do the Old Order Mennonites, who dress in distinctive clothes and drive horses and buggies, have in common with an urban Mennonite fellowship whose members drink only fair-trade coffee and have recently ordained a woman as their pastor? Where do the Conservative Mennonites or the Wisler Mennonites or the Beachy Amish fit into the larger picture?

Given the variety of these small Mennonite groups, it is not surprising that people are sometimes confused as to just who the Mennonites are or what they believe. Are Mennonites unusually divisive or cantankerous? Are they organizationally challenged? Would better theological training help them become more systematic and organized in their statements of faith?

Not necessarily. Mennonites are reluctant to structure the church around a hierarchy of leaders not because we are unsophisticated in our organization or unclear about our convictions.

Rather, Mennonites understand the church to consist of ordinary people, each of whom is responsible to read Scripture—in prayerful openness to the Spirit and in conversation with each other—and to seek God's will in concrete and specific ways. All members, not just trained theologians and bishops, share the task of reading God's Word, discerning its meaning for the contemporary church, and applying it to our daily lives. The interpretation of Scripture is the ongoing task of a living church, whose members continually seek to discern God's will within a changing cultural context.

Taking as its point of reference the Mennonite Church USA (the largest of the Mennonite groups in North America), this book sketches a basic *framework* for ongoing conversations about faithful discipleship within Mennonite congregations. But I do not pretend to summarize the full range of that further discussion.

Jazz musicians might appreciate the creative potential inherent in such an approach. When a jazz ensemble gathers to make music, each member needs to know the key signature and the basic chord progression; both are crucial if they are going to play well together. Beyond that, however, an accomplished jazz musician rarely expects the music of a given song to be written out note by note. In fact, it is precisely the anticipation of new, musical surprises that gives jazz its creative and pleasing quality. At the same time, jazz is not a celebration of absolute freedom or musical anarchy. If any of the musicians would suddenly shift keys or play an altogether different chord progression, the beauty of the music disappears and the efforts of the ensemble are thwarted.

Or consider another, more concrete, illustration of the way Mennonites express a shared theological unity beneath their apparent diversity. Every year, in nearly fifty different communities across the United States and Canada, a variety of Mennonite-related groups join together to organize a Mennonite relief sale. The relief sale is a collective ritual, often held at a local fairground, that on first appearance looks like a colorful folk festival. Hundreds, sometimes thousands, of people gather from far and wide to enjoy homemade food, local music, athletic events, and craftwork made by artisans from around the world. Although each sale has its distinctive characteristics, the high point of the event is usually a quilt auction, where bidders compete for a stunning array of finely stitched handcrafted quilts, all of them donated by local individuals or congregations. The proceeds from these sales—usually amounting to over four million (U.S.) dollars annually—support the Mennonite Central Committee, a relief and service organization devoted to alleviating poverty and suffering around the world. So at one level, relief sales are a highly effective means of raising funds for a denominational agency.

But at a deeper level the gatherings offer a wonderful insight into the nature and substance of Mennonite theology. Many relief sales include a public worship service of prayer and thanksgiving, usually highlighted by lots of singing, in which Mennonite groups of all sorts join with other Christians to raise their voices in praise to God. These are occasions to openly celebrate God's bounty and to remind us of our dependence on God's sustaining love.

But the worship service, and all of the activities that follow, are also a celebration of the gathered community. The sale is a cooperative event that relies heavily on volunteer labor and the contributions of hundreds of people. The animated conversations in the serving lines and crowded jostling in the auction barn remind everyone in attendance that they are all connected to each other and to a much larger body of Christian believers that extends far beyond the local congregation.

Relief sales also celebrate the gift of tradition and memory: quilts, ethnic food, and the sturdy wooden toys that are sold at the sale connect those in attendance with a generation that has gone before. The sale honors practices and skills from an earlier time, linking past and future generations.

Because the sales are organized around the explicit goal of supporting international relief efforts, they provide local Mennonite groups with a clear and tangible way of linking their faith to Christian service. The motto of Mennonite Central Committee states: "A cup of cold water offered in the name of Christ." Similarly, the money raised by the sale reminds Mennonites that responsibility for the neighbor extends to all who are suffering and in need, even beyond the boundaries of our own nation. And the highly visible handcrafts from around the world are a tangible reminder of the gifts that others have to offer us.

By themselves, these annual relief sales are not an adequate summary of Mennonite faith and practice (some might question, for example, the logic of an event where people come to buy and eat in order to help others who are impoverished or hungry!). Mennonites know that salvation cannot be earned by doing good deeds. We recognize that we are, from beginning to end, sustained by God's mercy and grace, utterly dependent on God for all that we have. But precisely because we have been the recipients of God's love, Mennonites feel compelled—joyfully—not only to speak about God's generous gift of forgiveness and love, but also to give concrete expression to that generosity by extending it to others.

All this brings me back to my conversation with the Japanese neighbor. A Mennonite approach to that conversation would need to include a summary of the basic convictions of the Christian church. A confession of faith about the doctrines we hold to be true must be part of our testimony to the world. But at the same time, it would be virtually impossible for my friend to truly understand the transforming power of Christian faith until he has seen and experienced God's love in action. Hence, to fully answer his question, I would need to invite my new friend to live and work for a time within a community of practicing Christians. For a Mennonite, the doctrines of the church become meaningful only in the context of particular expressions of faith lived out in action.

3

Interpreting Scripture

Through a Mennonite Lens

*You must know that God spoke to the Jews through Moses
and the prophets in a hidden manner. But when Christ himself
came, he and his apostles illuminated all things with a much
clearer understanding. Christ said quite openly that the law and
the prophets are summed up in these two commandments:
Love God with your whole heart, and your neighbor as yourself.*
—LEONARD SCHIEMER

*In the beginning was the Word, and
the Word was with God, and the Word was God.*
—JOHN 1:1

Bound between two ancient, leather-covered wood panels, the massive Bible weighs nearly fifteen pounds. Since its publication almost five centuries ago, successive generations of Mennonite owners have inscribed a long series of names in the flyleaf. Their scrawled signatures and notations of births, baptisms, marriages, and deaths are a clear testimony to the book's central place in the family household. The paper is still in excellent condition, though the edges are worn at the places where thumb and forefinger grasped and turned the pages.

Published in 1531 in Zurich by the printing family of

Christopher Froschauer, this Bible—along with other editions of the same translation—was eventually banned by Swiss authorities for its close association with Anabaptists. But Froschauer translations of the Bible, printed in secret, continued to find wide circulation among Mennonites in Switzerland and South Germany. Amazingly, dozens of these Bibles survived the dangerous Atlantic crossing from Europe to North America and they can still be found in Mennonite homes across the eastern part of the United States.

Christians today, of course, have come to regard the Bible as a household resource, available in dozens of customized versions and readily at hand, like the phone book or an encyclopedia, to consult when you find yourself in a crisis or needing answers to a specific question. For people living in the sixteenth century, however, access to the Scriptures marked a new era of freedom and possibility. Between 1516 and 1550, nearly thirty new translations of the Bible appeared in Europe, in dozens of different editions, many of them purchased by eager readers as fast as they appeared.

This new availability of the Scriptures was made possible, in part, by several revolutionary changes in technology. The introduction of moveable type during the last half of the fifteenth century, combined with more efficient and inexpensive ways of producing paper, enabled printers to produce mass quantities of books and pamphlets at a relatively affordable price. For a new class of entrepreneurs, publishing and selling Bibles was a commercial venture with the potential promise of enormous profits. For the Reformers of the early sixteenth century, access to the Bible was the source of power, the fulcrum for leveraging a thoroughgoing overhaul of the medieval Roman Catholic church.

Sola Scriptura—Scripture Alone

Tradition has it that on October 31, 1517, a young German monk by the name of Martin Luther nailed a document to the door of the main church in Wittenberg, and with that act ushered in a new era of history known as the Reformation. The document Luther posted—his so-called 95 Theses—argued that certain practices in the medieval Catholic church could not be justified on the basis of Scripture. In the years that followed, Luther's criticism of the church became more radical, as did his insistence that the Bible serve as the final authority in all theological or spiritual matters. "*Sola scriptura*," Luther insisted; "Scripture alone" was to be the final authority for Christian faith and practice.

To modern ears, the idea that Scripture should serve as the basis for the Christian life seems obvious. But in the sixteenth century such a claim threatened to undermine a monopoly on Scripture that authorities in the Catholic church had claimed for more than a thousand years. The Catholic church of the Middle Ages was obviously not opposed to the study of the Bible—far from it. But from long experience its leaders knew that Scripture could be interpreted in many different ways. If *everyone*—including barely literate peasants and shoemakers—suddenly began to read and interpret Scripture for themselves, the result would almost certainly be chaos.

Therefore, they argued, the Bible should be approached cautiously and thoughtfully. Its meaning for Christians could be properly understood only through the lens of tradition (the accumulated wisdom of church fathers like Augustine of Hippo and Thomas Aquinas) and the filter of time itself. Thus, potentially confusing passages could be interpreted within a broader theological context.

It stood to reason that only ordained priests—those who were literate in the language of the Bible (Latin) and knowledgeable about the tradition—could be entrusted to interpret Scripture. Their training and their commitment to the broad interests of the church ensured that the sermons they preached would be in line with the received wisdom of the Catholic church. Ultimately, if a dispute should happen to arise over a question of interpretation or a point of doctrine, the final word rested with the pope.

Luther and the other reformers of the early sixteenth century found these restrictions on Scripture intolerable. This monopoly on the right to interpret the Bible, they insisted, was merely a strategy of the Catholic church to maintain control over the masses. Bowing to the authority of tradition meant that all theological debates would always be decided in favor of the pope even before the discussion had even begun.

So when Luther set out to translate the Bible into the common German of his day, and when he insisted that theological questions could be resolved by appeal to "Scripture alone," he was challenging head-on the authority of the Catholic church. No longer was God's Word to be restricted only to those who could read Latin. Now, thanks to Luther's translation and the revolutionary technology of the printing press, virtually every literate person in Europe could study the Bible in their own language and in the privacy of their home. Suddenly, it seemed, the genie was out of the bottle. All over Europe, ordinary people began to read Scripture and to earnestly apply its message to their lives. People read the Bible hungrily, eagerly searching for fresh meanings to biblical stories or for new insights from the teachings of Jesus or the writings of the apostles.

The Challenge of Biblical Interpretation

During the earliest phase of the Reformation, Luther believed that God's truth was so clearly revealed in the Bible that no real interpretation was necessary. All that the sincere Christian needed to do was to read the Scripture and allow God's Word to be heard. "I acknowledge no fixed rules for the interpretation of the Word of God," he thundered in a letter of 1520 addressed to Pope Leo X, "since the Word of God, which teaches freedom in all matters, must not be bound."

In theory, that principle sounds just fine. Indeed, many non-denominational churches today insist that they believe only what the Bible says, without any "rules of interpretation." Unfortunately, however, as the reformers were quick to discover, the principle of "Scripture alone" is much easier to claim than to actually apply. Scripture passages that seem so plain to one reader can often be understood in dramatically different ways by other readers.

For many readers this new, direct encounter with Scriptures seemed to tap into an almost explosive power, offering an exhilarating and life-changing experience. Some peasants, for example, frustrated by generations of political inequity and economic injustice, discovered biblical themes of liberation and justice that seemed to apply exactly to their circumstances. Surely God would bless their demands for fairness and equality, even if it required a revolution. Others were fascinated by the prophetic books of Daniel and Revelation and traveled about proclaiming to anxious listeners that the end times were at hand. Still others took to heart the words of Jesus in the Sermon on the Mount and began to promote economic sharing and renounce the use of violence and the swearing of feudal loyalty oaths.

The Anabaptists were among the many groups in the sixteenth century who shared Luther's initial excitement about freeing Scripture from its captivity to the Latin language and the Catholic church's tight control over its interpretation. Like the reformers, they regarded the Bible as the Word of God, the foundation of faithful Christian life. Indeed, some early Anabaptists actively contributed to a translation of Scripture. Others composed a concordance of key biblical passages that continued to be reprinted for the next two centuries. Lay leaders committed large portions of Scripture to memory and Anabaptist writings are infused with biblical references. In dozens of courtroom interrogations and formal debates, they promised to submit to the authority of Scripture; if prosecutors could prove their arguments on the basis of the Bible, Anabaptists repeatedly insisted, they would gladly change their minds and repent of their errors.

Scripture Alone? The Reformers Retreat

Clearly, the principle of Scripture alone was useful for Luther in his struggle against the Catholic church. But he had not anticipated that people would use the same principle to defend all kinds of strange—and, in his view, heretical—teachings. As the unsettling consequences of this possibility became clear, he and other reformers like Zwingli and Calvin quickly retreated from their earlier conviction that the meaning of Scripture would be self-evident. They began to introduce tighter control over the teaching and interpreting of the Bible. Scripture could stay in the language of the people, they reasoned, but it needed to be understood through responsible filters such as catechisms, commentaries, and confessions of faith. Moreover, actual instruction from the Bible should be restricted to those pastors or ministers who had been properly trained in theology and formally authorized for this important task by the ritual of ordination. By the mid-1520s, Luther, who once made it known that he would accept no rules for interpreting Scripture, was well on his way to developing a set of clear criteria for reading the Bible, criteria that looked much like the rules he had earlier deplored.

At the heart of this tension, of course, is the challenge of interpretation. Few serious Christians question the authority of the Bible itself. But precisely because Scripture is so central to our understanding of God's will, Christians have frequently been divided over the much more difficult question of *how* Scripture should be correctly interpreted. Who, for example, are the people best qualified to interpret Scripture? What is the relationship of the Old Testament to the New Testament? How are contemporary believers to make sense of Paul's letters addressing first-century issues in churches scattered around the Mediterranean? How should Christians balance passages that seem in tension—or even in contradiction—with each other? Who should have the final word when confusion about the meaning of Scripture persists? What is the connection between Scripture, doctrine, and practice?

Over time, Christian groups inevitably develop principles for biblical interpretation (what biblical scholars call hermeneutics) that greatly influence their understanding of many other theological principles. Indeed, the principles for interpreting Scripture often reveal a great deal about the deeper convictions and assumptions of a particular group. In our survey of Mennonite beliefs, it is appropriate to start here, since Mennonite convictions about biblical interpretation shape the terrain of much of the material that follows.

A Mennonite Understanding of Scripture

1. The Bible Is Central to the Christian Life. From their beginnings, Mennonites have regarded the Bible as the foundation of a true understanding of Christian faith and practice. Like other Protestant reformers, the Anabaptists of the sixteenth century were committed to a path of church renewal that was grounded in Scripture alone. The Anabaptists gathered regularly for biblical study. They insisted that all theological questions be resolved solely on the basis of Scripture. And they often committed large portions of Scripture to memory. The language and stories of the Bible infuse Anabaptist hymns. Their written testimonies, prayers, and confessions are rich in biblical imagery.

Mennonites begin the journey of faith grounded in the clear conviction that Scripture is the Word of God, the baseline that informs all of Christian life. "Let no one remove you from the foundation which is laid through the letter of the holy Scriptures," wrote Michael Sattler shortly before his execution, "for it is sealed with the blood of Christ and of many witnesses of Jesus."

2. The Interpreting Community: Scripture Belongs to the Church. Recognizing that Scripture can be interpreted in various ways, Mennonites believe that the Bible should be read and interpreted collectively by the whole congregation—lay and ordained members alike. The Bible properly belongs to all Christian believers and should be accessible to everyone. Although the Anabaptists did have itinerant preachers, their earliest congregations were often led in study by lay readers whose primary task was to read Scriptures aloud and to then invite members of the group to reflect together on the meaning of the passage. This commitment to a participatory process of interpretation reflects the Anabaptist-Mennonite conviction that God's deepest desires for the Christian life are not mysterious or hidden. Those who come to Scripture earnestly seeking understanding will not return empty-handed, provided that the person is open to the presence of the Spirit, receptive to the collective wisdom of the congregation, and prepared to act on what the group discerns. While Mennonites are certainly not opposed to private devotions or to exegetical sermons, they understand the real work of interpreting to be a shared process of reading, reflecting, discussing, and discerning that involves the whole congregation.

3. The New Testament Interprets the Old Testament: A Christocentric Reading of Scripture. In the practical matter of how Scripture should be interpreted, most Mennonites groups have developed a set of general principles to untangle some of the internal tensions or confusing passages that appear in the Bible. Mennonites, for example, are generally inclined to trust the plain, or more literal, reading of Scripture over a more complex interpretation, especially if the more complex reading moves in the direction of blunting the radical edge of Christ's call to discipleship. They tend to be cautious about a preoccupation with prophetic texts like Daniel and Revelation. From historical experience they have learned how easy it is for congregations to be led astray by charismatic preachers who claim special insight into the hidden meanings of these passages.

Probably the most important principle of interpretation, however, is a basic distinction between the Old Testament—with its themes of promise, law, and warfare—and the New Testament, with its parallel motifs of fulfillment, grace, and self-giving love. In making this distinction Mennonites are not suggesting that the Old Testament is irrelevant. But followers of Christ are participants in the New Covenant, part of a movement in history so profoundly different from what came before that the Western tradition reset its calendar to mark the new beginning! Jesus himself explicitly underscored the differences between the Old and New Covenant: "You have heard it was said . . . ," Jesus repeatedly instructs his listeners in the Sermon on the Mount, referring to the law of the Old Testament. "But I tell you . . . ," he continues as he challenges his followers to pursue a new, higher, standard of moral behavior that would characterize his new kingdom (as in Matt 5:43-44).

Thus, Christ's followers are called beyond loving their neighbors—which is what every human social code expects—to love their enemies as well. The Old Testament is clear that you should not commit adultery; Jesus goes further to call his disciples to not even think lustful thoughts, but to regard everyone with dignity and respect. The same holds true of possessions. Instead of giving each person their due ("an eye for an eye, and a tooth for a tooth"), Jesus teaches his followers to give freely and lavishly beyond what might be expected.

This commitment to reading Scripture through the lens of Christ—what is sometimes called a Christocentric approach to Scripture—is a recognition that Jesus is the final standard for the Christian believer. Thus, all of Scripture, both the Old and New Testaments, should be interpreted in a way that is consistent with the revelation of God in Jesus Christ.

This conviction has sometimes led opponents to accuse Mennonites of ignoring the Old Testament altogether, a charge the Anabaptists also faced and earnestly refuted. The Old Testament is a valuable resource for the Christian. It tells the story of God's saving acts and establishes the criteria for the coming of the Messiah. At the same time, however, Mennonites believe that Christians find the fullest revelation of God's nature and God's will for the world in Jesus.

Therefore, we read the Old Testament through the lens of the New Testament. If teachings from the Old Testament are ever in conflict with those of the New Testament, the latter takes priority as the highest revelation of God's will for humanity. "I accept the Old Testament wherever it points to Christ," argued the Anabaptist Hans Pfistermeyer. "However, Christ came with a more exalted and perfect teaching. He showed his people a new covenant which they would need if their righteousness were to exceed that of the scribes and hypocrites."

This principle became particularly relevant in the controversy sparked by the Anabaptist teachings against the oath, infant baptism, and the use of violence. In all of these instances, the Anabaptists took as their starting point the teachings of Jesus. Their opponents, by contrast, often sought to qualify Christ's teachings on these points by pointing to texts in the Old Testament that seemed to justify oath-swearing, infant baptism, or the sword.

4. A Book for Life: We Study the Bible to Become Disciples. In a similar way, the Anabaptist-Mennonite tradition has insisted that the teachings of Scripture—particularly those of Jesus—were actually meant to be followed. Part of the Anabaptist suspicion of academic theology was its tendency to develop sophisticated arguments for avoiding the plain and simple meaning of the text. The Bible was not given by God to be debated, but to be lived. This means that we don't study Scripture as an intellectual exercise, but out of a hunger to discern God's will. Thus, Mennonite principles of interpretation are closely linked to a life of faithful obedience. Scripture—especially the teachings of Christ in the New Testament —is a living text, to be studied as the standard for daily Christian life, even if some of Jesus's more radical teachings seem to go against natural reason, church tradition, or political self-interest.

To argue, as did the Anabaptists, that Jesus's words in Scripture were to be understood and practiced literally was profoundly unsettling. It challenged many of the practices of the institutional church. It portrayed the institutions of Christendom as corrupt and hypocritical. And it opened the door to radical understandings of economics and power that could become a blueprint for social reorganization.

5. Beyond the Safety of Formula: Biblical Interpretation as an Ongoing Process. While Mennonites held to a very high view of Scripture, with a strong emphasis on obedience to the literal teachings of Jesus, most also recognized the danger of a legalism that reduced Scripture to a dead letter. Thus, Mennonites, and the Anabaptists before them, distinguish the Outer Word (the external realities of preaching, baptism, and reading the Bible) from the Inner Word (the activity of the Holy Spirit at work in the soul of each human being). Both are necessary for a proper understanding of God's will. God speaks in both the Outer Word of Scripture as well as in the Inner Word of revelation. But either one can easily be stressed to the detriment of the other.

A focus on the Outer Word alone can quickly become legalistic and oppressive, a tool of the powerful who use the Bible as a weapon. On the other hand, those inclined to private visions and subjective claims of prophetic insight in their charismatic power. It is the task of the congregation to be attentive to both the external word of Scripture and the inner movement of the Spirit.

In Scripture, the church has a sure source of God's intention for humanity. But since we now "see but a poor reflection" (1 Cor 13:12), we need the constant insight of the larger community and the presence of the Spirit to rightly discern God's will.

4

Interpreting Scripture

A Critique... and Ongoing Questions

For many modern readers these Mennonite principles of biblical interpretation may not seem all that revolutionary. But in the sixteenth century, Catholic and Protestant authorities alike found these understandings, and the ethical practices that followed from them, deeply unsettling. In their public debates and courtroom interrogations, at least three major concerns repeatedly surfaced. Although contemporary Christians are less inclined to use the language of heresy, these concerns continue to emerge as modern Mennonites engage in ecumenical conversations with other Christians.

1. A Community Approach to Reading the Bible Will Lead to Anarchy. As the Protestant reformers began to recognize that the principle of Scripture alone could lead in many different directions, they quickly implemented safeguards to prevent individuals from preaching doctrines that they regarded as heresy. Both the Lutheran and the Reformed tradition, for example, soon introduced a preaching office that limited biblical instruction to a trained clergy, formally ordained to carry out this task. Both traditions also developed carefully worded confessions of faith (the Augsburg Confession for the Lutherans and the Heidelberg Catechism for the Reformed) that served as an official lens through which Scripture was to be correctly interpreted. And both traditions, in keeping with the medieval blending of religion and politics, recognized that the state had a strong interest in repressing any interpretation of Scripture that could lead to social unrest. Among Lutherans, for example, the territorial prince became the highest bishop (*summus episcopus*) of the church. For their part, Reformed theologians assumed that the local city council would play a significant role in shaping the public life of the church.

For most of the reformers, the idea of involving lay members of the church in biblical interpretation was both naive and dangerous. On the one hand, it granted illiterate, untrained artisans and peasants as much voice in interpreting the complex meanings of Scripture as the person who had spent a lifetime studying the biblical languages and reflecting on theological issues. What possible good could come from encouraging common, ordinary, laypeople— ignorant of the biblical languages and the rich theological tradition of the church fathers—to debate about the Scriptures? Such an approach was an invitation to interpretive anarchy. In the words of the stalwart Catholic Thomas More, it simply "granted to every individual the freedom to chart his own path to Hell."

Equally troubling were the potential social and political consequences of throwing the Scriptures open to everyone. Here the authorities had some basis for their fears. On various occasions in the sixteenth century, small groups of Anabaptists did get caught up in extremist interpretations. One group in the Netherlands, for example, reportedly played with toys in the public square in an effort to literally enact Christ's teaching that only those who became "like children" could enter the kingdom of God. More seriously, a group of Anabaptists in the north German city of Münster gathered around the apocalyptic preaching of several self-proclaimed prophets in anticipation of the second coming of Christ. Before an army finally brought an end to their short-lived kingdom, several hundred people lost their lives in an Anabaptist-inspired reign of terror.

Acknowledging the danger of private revelations, Mennonites have been appropriately sobered by these examples of eccentric behavior. But the antidote to both silly interpretation and apocalyptic excess, they have argued, is precisely a community-centered approach to Scripture reading, in which various teachings are continually tested by the group wisdom of the congregation. To turn the interpretation of Scripture over to political authorities or an educated minority of theological elites meant that Scripture would once again be held captive to institutional interests.

2. The Mennonite Emphasis on Following Christ Leads to Legalism.

While the seriousness with which Mennonites approach the teachings of Jesus might seem admirable, closer examination makes it clear, at least to many Protestant theologians, that this preoccupation with ethics is naive and spiritually dangerous. It is naive in the sense that no Christian, Mennonite or otherwise, can ever literally follow Christ's teachings in the Sermon on the Mount. Not even the most selfless Christians "give to all who ask" (Matt 5:42). Even the most trusting believers occasionally "give thought for the morrow" (Matt 6:34) when they enter an appointment in their day planners. And few Christians are ready to "gouge out" their eye if it causes them to sin (Matt 5:29).

In other words, even those Christians who claim that Christ's teachings are to be followed literally eventually apply some principle of interpretation that moves away from a literal application of the text. In the end, Mennonites, like all other Christians, follow Jesus's teachings selectively.

But the real problem with the Mennonite emphasis on ethics goes to an even deeper theological issue: the question of grace and works. We will pick up this question in more detail in later chapters, but with regard to biblical interpretation, Martin Luther was clear that the theological principle of grace should inform our understanding of Christ's teachings regarding ethical behavior. Teachings like the Sermon on the Mount are part of the larger structure of law (commandments to be obeyed) that runs throughout Scripture. The purpose of the law, beginning with the Ten Commandments, is to point Christians to the righteousness of God. The law reminds us that we stand before a holy God, who demands obedience. At the same time, however, anyone who examines their life honestly will be forced to acknowledge over and over again how far short we come in actually living up to the standard of the law.

Thus, the law—and especially the standards of perfection that Jesus seems to be holding up in the Sermon on the Mount—serves a very important function. But that function, according to Luther and many other Protestants, is primarily to drive us to despair as we recognize our inability to live according to its standards. And precisely in the moment of despair, we encounter God's free gift of grace. Nothing in the teachings of Jesus was intended as a blueprint for the church or human relations more generally. Instead, the focus of Scripture is on the redemptive work of Christ: his salvation on the cross and the free gift of grace offered on our behalf.

When faced with these arguments, the Anabaptist generally responded by returning to what they called "the plain and simple teachings of Jesus." "Yes," they agreed, "we humans are ultimately saved by God's grace and not by our good deeds." However, they also noted numerous passages throughout Scripture where God's promise of blessing is clearly *conditioned* on the human response. Indeed, the Lord's Prayer even makes God's forgiveness of our sins explicitly contingent on our willingness to forgive others: "*If* you do not forgive [others] their sins, your Father will not forgive your sins" (Matt 6:12, 14-15).

Mennonites do not see Christ's teachings as a rule book or as an encyclopedia with an answer for every ethical question we might face. But taking Scripture seriously means to be prepared, by the empowering grace of God and the Holy Spirit, to live in accordance with the path of Jesus, even if that means going against the grain of the culture around us. We may not always agree on every specific detail, but this should be an impetus to more careful thinking and discernment, not an argument— or an excuse—to give up on the call to holiness.

3. The Mennonite Emphasis on the New Testament Leads to Confusion About the Character of God. Some critics, especially from the Reformed tradition, have raised other questions about the Mennonite understanding of the relationship between the Old Testament and the New Testament. As we will see in later chapters, Christ's teachings on nonviolence and love of the enemy are central to Mennonite theology. But what about the many examples of righteous violence and holy warfare in the Old Testament? Repeatedly, God not only tolerated war in the Old Testament, but even commanded the Israelites to fight on his behalf. Occasionally God actually punished them for not being violent enough in their defeat of the enemy. Is this the same God who, in the New Testament, appears to renounce violence? If so, it would seem that Mennonites are put into an awkward position. If they aren't going to ignore these parts of the Old Testament altogether, then they either are suggesting that God's nature changed from the Old Testament era to the New Testament, or that Jesus did not represent the full character of God. Both options seem to verge on the heretical.

Here again, Mennonites have generally responded with simple affirmations rather than with highly sophisticated theological arguments. They begin by noting that the revelation of God in Christ marks a fundamental break in human history, a moment so significant that we reset our calendars around the year of Christ's birth. Since Jesus is the fullest and most complete revelation of God's character and God's will for humanity, his followers no long regard themselves as Old Testament Jews (identified with the law of Moses), but as Christians (literally, "little Christs"). The intention here is not to disregard the Old Testament but to ask, as Jesus did, what it might mean to "fulfill" the law by treating all humans with dignity and love, regardless of the cost. "We confess," said an Anabaptist to a group of Reformed theologians in 1532, "that the Old Testament is a witness to Christ. Further, we grant it validity wherever Christ has not suspended it and wherever it agrees with the New. We consider it right and good if it serves faith, love, and a good Christian life."

Mennonites may also note that the theological conundrum of the apparent shift in God's nature from the Old to the New Testaments is not resolved by simply citing Old Testament examples where God appears to sanction violence. In the New Testament, Jesus—God incarnate—clearly rejects the notion of holy war and, indeed, commands his followers to love their enemies (Matt 5:44). Hence, those who insist that God's character never changes are confronted with exactly the same theological question that they insist is so problematic for Christian pacifists. In response to this apparent dilemma, most Mennonites would say that God has not changed in his essential character. What has changed, however, are human understandings of God's desire for us to live in complete harmony and trust with him and with each other. That desire, which has *always* been a part of God's character, has now been made unmistakably clear in the life, teaching, death, and resurrection of Jesus.

Ongoing Questions for Mennonites Today

1. Do Mennonites Believe in the Inerrancy of Scripture? "All Scripture," we read in the epistle to Timothy, "is God-breathed and is useful for teaching, rebuking, correcting and training in righteousness" (2 Tim 3:16). When the apostle Paul wrote those words, he was almost certainly referring to the Hebrew Scriptures, what Christians today call the Old Testament. But Christians have justifiably claimed this description of Scripture as "breathed of God" (or "in-spired") and "useful for teaching" as applicable to the New Testament as well.

Still, Mennonites have not always been in absolute agreement about what this means. Some Mennonites, influenced by American Fundamentalism, have insisted on a strict formulation about the authority of Scripture that would include words like inerrant, plenary, and verbally inspired. In this view, the Bible is of a single piece. To question the literal truth of any single verse inevitably calls into question the integrity of the whole.

However, many Mennonites, probably the majority, would not hold to such a strict view of Scripture. They would be more likely to read Scriptures inductively, seeking to understand the context of a given passage, and then to translate the meaning of that teaching from its biblical setting to the modern day.

More generally, Mennonites tend to regard the Bible as a record of God's actions in history (salvation history). It offers a clear description of the human condition; it documents God's revelation in Jesus Christ; and it calls us to participate with God's purposes in history as they continue to be worked out. Thus, Scripture is the inspired (God-breathed) record of God's active presence in the world, and it is "useful for teaching, rebuking, correcting and training in righteousness." But this need not imply that the authority of the Bible depends on its accuracy in every detail of history, biology, or astronomy. The Bible is a window through which we can see God. Those who seek the truth in its pages will not be disappointed.

2. The Idea of an Interpreting Community Sounds Good, But Is It Actually Practiced? It is true that the lived reality within many Mennonite congregations is often far less consistent than their stated ideals. Reading and interpreting Scripture collectively is a labor-intensive and time-consuming process. In our fragmented and busy lives, it is often difficult to set aside adequate time for personal Bible study and for patient conversation with each other about what the Scriptures might be telling us today. Moreover, Mennonites, like most Protestant churches, now generally rely on seminary-trained pastors to preach their sermons. The professional pastorate has brought enormous benefits to the Mennonite church; but it has also had the indirect effect of encouraging laypeople to allow their paid staff (those with training in theology and the biblical languages) to bear most of the load when it comes to biblical study. And then there is the reality of individualism in modern culture and the high value that we often place on personal feelings and experiences. As a result, fewer people today are inclined to regard the collective voice of the congregation as having immediate authority over their personal choices.

Still, elements of the interpreting community live on in the Mennonite church. Drawing on an older tradition in which one or two members of the congregation routinely offered a formal comment on the sermon by "bearing witness" (*Zeugnis*), many Mennonite congregations continue to designate a time for sharing following the sermon. Members are invited to offer perspectives on the sermon, and to do so in public, rather than just privately around the dinner table. Often this is an occasion to reflect on how the sermon applies to personal circumstances. But the opportunity for responding also serves as a reminder that the preacher does not necessarily have the final word.

On a somewhat larger scale, it is worth noting that the Mennonite church took nearly ten years to complete its most recent confession of faith as it circulated the document in various stages back to congregations and individuals for their critical comments. Although the final result did not meet with 100 percent approval, the process was clearly collaborative and consensual. In this and other matters, Mennonite congregations are generally inclined to decision making by consensus, taking the time to solicit broad affirmation from the community, rather than pursuing a straightforward majority rule approach.

3. What Happens When Mennonites Just Cannot Agree? Mennonites have not been immune to the debates over biblical interpretation that have sometimes divided denominations. In retrospect, it is sometimes difficult to fully appreciate why some issues were so divisive. In the late nineteenth century, for example, some Mennonite churches split over the introduction of four-part singing (now a beloved, seemingly timeless, characteristic of North American Mennonite identity). Other contentious issues were the shift from German to English as the language of worship and the introduction of Sunday schools and revival meetings. In each of these instances, new understandings sparked intense conversations both in local congregations and more broadly at the denominational level. After a time of discussion, the church found a way to accommodate the change, though often at the expense of several congregations leaving the denomination. This was the case again around the middle of the twentieth century when one part of the Mennonite church gradually dropped the devotional covering, or prayer veiling, that had long been a part of the traditional dress for a significant number of Mennonite women. And a similar pattern could be seen a decade or two later over the question of women in pastoral leadership roles or the remarriage of members who had been divorced.

Currently, some members of the Mennonite church are engaged in a debate regarding biblical understandings of homosexuality. After a lengthy period of study, the denomination as a whole issued a statement that did not recommend changes in the traditional understanding regarding homosexuality and marriage. Yet the church did commit itself to continued conversation and challenged congregations to regard homosexually oriented members in their midst as Christians in good standing, as long as they remained celibate. As in earlier debates over biblical interpretation, some congregations have opted to leave the Mennonite church. Most, however, affirm the church's teaching and are ready to redirect their energies to other matters.

4. What Translation of the Bible Do Mennonites Prefer? Fifty years ago most Mennonite congregations, like most churches in the United States, would have used the King James Version of the Bible. Although an older generation of Mennonites still prefers the formal speech of the King James Version, with its thees and thous along with the familiar cadences of the Psalms and other passages committed to memory, they would be in a clear minority. In general, we have not been inclined to link the authority of scripture to a single translation.

Today, Mennonites use a wide variety of translations, with the New International Version predominating among many congregations. A growing number of Mennonites have also turned to the New Revised Standard Version, especially in public worship, in light of its measured concession to gender-neutral language. Mennonites are appreciative of the insights brought to bear by scholars who have learned to read the original Hebrew and Greek, but they have little sense that reading the Bible in the original language carries with it any unique authority.

5. What Do Mennonites Believe About Other, Nonbiblical, Sources of Truth? Mennonites have inherited a legacy of practical faith that values the application of Scripture in daily life over abstract reflection on knotty theological issues. They tend to have a high level of confidence that thoughtful study, combined with prayer for the Spirit's leading and the collective wisdom of the community, will be sufficient to orient Christians to the will of God. Although Mennonites are not explicitly hostile to human reason as a source of moral authority, they are not inclined to rely heavily on arguments from natural law or the order of creation in their ethics and theology. To be sure, Paul speaks in Romans (2:15) about a law, common to all human beings, that is "written on our hearts." But Paul also declares that the story of Christ crucified is "foolishness to Gentiles" (1 Cor 1:23). Jesus calls us to a way of life that seems, at least on the surface, to transcend the arguments of natural reason. Ethical reasoning based on "the order of creation" (the "nature of things") is often used to justify the status quo of the fallen world. Yet Jesus came proclaiming that he was "making everything new" (cf. Luke 5:36-39; Rev 21:5). So in our interpretation of Scripture, Mennonites are not opposed to reason or to drawing insights from creation. But we are eager to distinguish descriptions about what "is" from the call of Jesus that orients us to what "ought" to be.

Summary

As we have seen, Mennonites share with the broader Christian tradition a very high view of Scripture and a conviction that the

Bible is indeed the Word of God, authoritative in matters of faith and practice. The bigger challenge to Christian unity has less to do with the authority of Scripture than with the principles for interpreting the Bible. How is the link made between the text and the daily life and experience of the Christian believer? Here Mennonites have inclined toward a cluster of interpretive practices that have sometimes set us at odds with other Christians.

We are Christocentric in our reading of the Bible—more inclined to regard the teachings of the New Testament as authoritative for Christian life than those in the Old Testament and quick to turn to the authority of Jesus when difficult questions of interpretation arise. The Bible, Mennonites believe, is to be read and interpreted by the congregation that is guided by the Holy Spirit, attentive to the changing realities of the culture, and open to the voices of dissenting perspectives. Above all, the Bible is a book of life and for life. In it, we hear God speaking and we discover God's will for daily living. Indeed, the two cannot finally be separated. In living our faith we encounter God, and in the encounter with God we find strength and joy for life.

5

Believers Baptism

Choosing Our King

On January 21, 1525, a small group of young men gathered secretly in a house near the center of the Swiss city of Zurich for an unusual worship service. Raised in the Catholic church, the men were now part of a movement for religious reform that was sharply critical of Catholic theology and practice. For several years they had been meeting for Bible study and discussion with their mentor, Ulrich Zwingli, the priest at the city's main church. Increasingly, they were convinced that several practices of the Catholic church—especially the mass, infant baptism, and the obligation to pay certain tithes— could not be defended on the basis of Scripture. But like many radical groups, they were not of one mind about the appropriate strategy for implementing their reforms. When Zwingli, in agree- ment with the Zurich City Council, insisted on a course of moderate reforms, introduced gradually, several members of his circle resisted. In their judgment, if the scriptural teaching was clear, the changes should be made immediately, no matter how radical and regardless of the broader political or social consequences. So on that January afternoon in 1525, this small group formally renounced their bap- tisms as infants and, in the pattern of Jesus and John the Baptist, received baptism as adults as a symbol of their conscious commitment to follow Christ and to support each other in this new step of faith.

For modern Christians, such an action is likely to strike us as almost trivial. Regardless of what one may believe about baptism, what could be so troubling about a group of people gathering for prayer and then pouring water over their heads? Yet this gesture— marking the beginning of the Anabaptist (re-baptizer) movement and, by extension, of the Mennonite church—had profound consequences, especially as the group dispersed and began to express their convictions in public settings. Within days, the Zurich City Council ordered the arrest and imprisonment of anyone who participated in such a baptism. By 1526, authorities declared the baptism of adults a capital offense. And in January of 1527, Felix Manz, in whose home the group had met, suffered the ultimate consequence of his convictions. With his hands and feet bound to a wooden pole, Manz was "baptized" once more as he was pushed into the icy waters of the Limmat River in a ceremony of public execution.

The Zurich authorities were not alone in their hostile reaction to this newly formed group. As the Anabaptist movement spread through Switzerland, southwestern Germany, and down the Rhine valley, Catholic princes and Protestant reformers alike condemned them as heretics and called for their execution. "The Anabaptists," wrote Martin Luther, are "false prophets" who sneak about the country like "wolves in sheep's clothing, deceiving the innocent." "They are mean-spirited, self-righteous, envious and judgmental, . . . a threat to social order," wrote Swiss reformer Ulrich Zwingli. They are "blasphemers," echoed Philipp Melanchthon, who "should be put to death." And John Calvin, sixteenth-century French reformer and founder of the Reformed church, called them "a plague and a pestilence."

This chapter explores the Mennonite understanding of baptism, focusing less on the actual ceremony itself than on the multilayered cluster of meanings that the act has come to symbolize. As with many Christians, baptism for Mennonites is closely linked to salvation.

But salvation in a Mennonite context is understood not so much as a ritual act (the rite of baptism itself) or as a single moment of decision (the precise date of giving one's heart to Jesus). Rather, Mennonites understand salvation more as a lifelong journey of faith characterized by several crucial ingredients: a spiritual relationship with God, a commitment to full participation in the community of faith, and a willingness to follow Jesus's teachings in daily life. Baptism symbolizes all of these things. Like a marriage vow, it is a serious—albeit joyful—public statement of commitment made in full awareness of the responsibilities and consequences implied in that vow. Thus, Mennonites believe that baptism should be reserved for those who are old enough to understand the nature of this decision and are ready to commit themselves fully to this journey of faith.

Baptism in the Christian Tradition

The ingredients seem simple enough: water, a gathering of witnesses, and a few carefully chosen words. To a secular person looking in from the outside, it might seem hard to understand why the Christian practice of baptism is so significant. Yet, despite its elemental simplicity, virtually every Christian denomination regards baptism as a foundational event, a ritual that embodies the essence of an entire theological tradition. Few practices are more central to the Christian church. And few have been the source of more disagreement and debate among Christians. Is baptism essential to salvation? When is the appropriate moment for baptism? Should the person being baptized be sprinkled or immersed? Does the very act of baptism confer salvation, or is baptism merely a symbol of salvation already received?

The roots of Christian baptism draw deeply on the images and stories of the Old Testament. Water, of course, has always been an elemental symbol of cleansing, refreshment, and life itself. We know of its destructive power in the story of the Flood, but more frequently water in the Old Testament is associated with God's healing presence. Water is a spring in the desert, a life-giving well, or justice that flows "like a mighty river." The symbol of Christian baptism comes to us directly from the Old Testament story of the exodus, when God parted the waters of the Red Sea to allow the children of Israel to escape from Pharaoh's pursuing armies and slavery in Egypt. That dramatic act of "crossing through the waters" marked a foundational moment in biblical history: the rebirth of the children of Israel. Now they were no longer downtrodden slaves of Pharaoh, but a new community of God's people, bound to each other by the gift of the law and by their daily dependence on God for guidance and sustenance.

Echoes of the exodus story can be clearly heard in the New Testament account of John, the forerunner of Jesus, who was nicknamed "the Baptist." John's fiery preaching called for repentance— a transformation of the heart symbolized by a ritual cleansing in the waters of the Jordan River. According to the Gospels, Jesus began his formal ministry only after he had been baptized by John. That act—accompanied by God's blessing and the clear presence of the Holy Spirit—marked a "crossing over" for Jesus into a new ministry of healing and teaching that ultimately culminated three years later in his crucifixion, death, and resurrection.

The early Christians understood baptism as a symbol rich with meanings drawn both from the Old Testament and from the life of Jesus. As with the exodus, baptism in the early church symbolized the renunciation of a life enslaved to the bondage of sin and a crossing over into a new identity within a community of believers who, like the children of Israel, were committed to living in dependence on God. But the early Christians also regarded baptism as a ritual reenactment of the death and resurrection of Christ. In some settings, the baptismal candidates walked into the water naked (stripped and vulnerable, like Christ on the cross, dying to the old self). After emerging from the water, they were dressed in robes of white as a symbol of the resurrection and their new identity as followers of Jesus. In each instance, however, the central themes are clear: a transformation of the heart; a commitment to a new life of discipleship to Jesus; and membership in a new community of believers.

Beyond these central themes the New Testament sources provide us with relatively few detailed instructions for the actual practice of baptism in the early church. Some traditions, for example, have cited Philip's baptism of the Ethiopian eunuch immediately following his confession of faith as a model for baptizing at the moment of conversion (Acts 8:38). Other groups have used the reference to the baptism of the Philippian jailor "and all his family" as a precedent for the baptism of infants and children (16:33).

Catholic and Protestant Understandings of Baptism

If the exact details of apostolic baptismal practice seem to have been somewhat fluid, strong evidence from the second and third centuries suggests that the early Christians baptized only adults. Baptism came only after a prolonged period of rigorous instruction and training. In other words, the early church reserved baptism for those who had demonstrated in word and practice that they were truly committed to becoming followers of Jesus.

Sometime during the fourth century, however, this practice of lengthy instruction (the catechumenate) had begun to change. At the heart of this shift in baptismal practice was the conversion of the Roman emperor Constantine in 312, a momentous event that slowly transformed the nature of the Christian church. During the century following Constantine's conversion to Christianity, the church went from being a small, persecuted minority, far removed from the center of political power, to becoming a powerful institution whose bishops came to rely on the armies of the Roman Empire both for their protection and as a means of eliminating heresy. Over time, membership in the Christian church shifted from a small gathering of courageous believers whose beliefs and practices were sharply at odds with the broader culture, to include virtually everyone who lived within the borders of the Roman Empire. This shift in Christian practice following Constantine's reign was never formulated quite this starkly. But the emerging consensus seemed clear: the Roman political authorities would cease persecuting Christians, and, indeed, would adopt Christianity as the official religion of the land. In return, Christians would become loyal subjects and Christian faith would serve as a kind of religious-cultural glue that could help to unite a fragmenting empire.

Inevitably, understandings of baptism began to shift as well. By the fifth century everyone within the territory was now compelled by law to be a Christian. Hence, it no longer made sense to associate baptism with repentance (a dramatic change in personal behavior) or with a new identity within a community of believers.

About the same time, new theological arguments began to emerge that encouraged this shift in the church's understanding toward the practice of infant baptism. For example, Augustine of Hippo (354-430), whose writings deeply shaped the trajectory of later Christian thought, insisted that human beings, from the very moment of their birth, were trapped in bondage to sin. Since the fall of Adam and Eve, he argued, sin is not a matter of human choice, but a genetic reality—we are born in sin. Thus, Augustine concluded, the baptism of infants is necessary for the salvation of the child's soul. Conversely, any who has not received the benefit of baptism is destined to hell.

Out of this argument emerged in Catholic theology the understanding of baptism as a *sacrament*—an action that extends a spiritual gift of grace by the very performance of the ritual. Thus, when a priest baptizes a newborn baby, the act itself literally confers salvation, so that the infant is saved from the stain of original sin and the clutches of hell. Through the ritual of baptism, the infant becomes a Christian. Parents can rest assured that his or her soul is saved and that their child has been incorporated into the church.

The political and theological consequences of infant baptism became foundational for medieval society. In a Christian culture where the lines between church and state were frequently indistinguishable, baptism formally marked the infant's status not only as a child of the church, but also as a member of the civic community.

Entering the infant's name on the baptismal roll identified the child as an eventual tax-paying subject, who would owe political allegiance to the local feudal lord.

The Reformation did little to challenge these basic practices. Both Lutheran and Calvinist reformers shared the medieval assumption that all of society is Christian (though they now defined the boundaries of the institutional church to be the same as that of each individual state). They agreed that infants should be baptized as soon after birth as possible. For most reformers, the point was so obvious that it scarcely needed to be defended. Luther, borrowing heavily from Augustine, argued that infant baptism underscores our dependence on God's grace for our salvation. Baptizing a passive, helpless, and utterly dependent baby makes it unmistakably clear that we are not saved by our own merits but by the free gift of God's forgiveness.

Ulrich Zwingli, the Swiss reformer, developed a slightly different argument for the practice of infant baptism. Noting that Jesus taught that we must become "like children" to enter the kingdom of God, he emphasized the significance of baptism as a means of incorporating the infant into the community of faith. Infant baptism, he insisted, serves Christians in the same way that circumcision did for the Jews of the Old Testament. Baptism became a sign of inclusion into the body of believers and a commitment on the part of believers to raise that child in the ways of God.

Though the theological arguments for infant baptism varied somewhat, Catholics and Protestants alike agreed that it was an essential Christian practice. Without it, the soul of the infant was imperiled and the child's civil status left unclear. Perhaps even more troubling, not baptizing infants would suggest that European society was divided into those who made a commitment of baptism (Christians) and those who had not (non-Christians). This was an almost unimaginable circumstance in a culture that understood itself to be thoroughly Christian. So when Anabaptist leaders began to challenge the principle of infant baptism, people reacted with understandable confusion, anger, and eventually, violence.

Anabaptist-Mennonite Understandings of Baptism

Biblical Basis for Believers Baptism. For Mennonites, the primary argument for believers baptism, as opposed to infant baptism, rests on a bedrock principle of the Reformation itself: Scripture alone. In their reading of the New Testament, the Anabaptists of the sixteenth century could find no scriptural justification for the practice of baptizing babies. Sometimes the Anabaptists cited the example of Jesus, who had not been baptized until the age of thirty. More typically, however, they referred to Jesus's teachings that explicitly link baptism with repentance and belief—things that an infant clearly is not capable of doing. While instructing the disciples to preach the good news of the gospel, for example, Jesus promises, "Whoever believes and is baptized will be saved" (Mark 16:16). Here the sequence seems clear: belief comes first, then baptism.

Similarly, at the end of his ministry, in a final admonition to the disciples known as the Great Commission, Jesus again speaks of baptism. "Therefore go," he told the disciples, "and make disciples of all nations, baptizing them in the name of the Father and of the Son and of the Holy Spirit, and teaching them to obey everything that I have commanded you" (Matt 28:19-20). Here again, the expected order of events does not seem accidental. Jesus commands his followers first to "make disciples," and then to baptize, with the expectation that the new converts should also be taught to obey Christ's commandments. In other words, people become followers of Jesus by hearing, understanding, and responding to a call—just as the first disciples had done.

"First," explained Anabaptist leader Hans Hut in language reminiscent of other testimony, "Christ said, Go forth into the whole world, preach the Gospel to every creature. Second, he said, Whosoever believes, and third, is baptized—the same shall be saved. This order must be maintained if a true Christianity is to be erected." This same sequence reoccurs in the story of the first baptisms of the apostolic church as recorded in Acts 2:14-41. The story begins with Peter preaching a sermon to a crowd of Jews who have gathered in Jerusalem for the annual celebration of the Pentecost. His proclamation of the gospel culminates with a call to repentance. "Those who accepted his message," the account concludes, "were baptized."

Thus, the New Testament model suggests that baptism follows naturally upon hearing the good news of the gospel, expressing an attitude of repentance, and opening oneself to receive God's gift of forgiveness and grace. For Mennonites, this teaching means that baptism results from a conscious decision—made only after the believer has genuinely recognized alternate claims of allegiance and is committed to following Jesus wholly and without reservation. Such a commitment implies a radical reorientation of priorities. As early Christians and Anabaptists alike experienced first hand, this was a decision that could lead to persecution and even death. A decision that significant could hardly be made by an infant, nor could anyone else make such a decision on the believer's behalf.

The Meaning of Baptism: A Three-Stranded Cord. Mennonites do not believe that the act of baptism, in itself, makes a person Christian—whether one is a baby or an adult. Baptism is therefore not a "sacrament" in the sense that it carries inherent spiritual power, but rather is a "sign" or a "symbol."

As we all know, symbols can have more than just one meaning. A flag, or the cross, or a wedding ring can each evoke a wide variety of images in our minds. This is one reason why these symbols are so powerful in our culture. In a similar way, baptism in the Mennonite tradition is a symbol that communicates several closely-related truths.

Drawing on a text from 1 John, the Anabaptists frequently described the meaning of baptism as a kind of three-stranded cord, an interweaving of several distinct themes that joined to make a unified whole. Children of God, we read in 1 John 5, are those who believe that Jesus is the Christ and follow his commandments. Three things, the writer continues, testify that Jesus is the Son of God: "the Spirit, the water and the blood; and the three are in agreement" (5:8). Within the Anabaptist-Mennonite tradition these three images—spirit, water, and blood—point to the essential truths of baptism, each equally dependent on the others for its meaning and power.

1. At its most basic level, baptism is a visible sign of the transforming presence of the Holy Spirit. Mennonites frequently refer to baptism as "an outward sign of an inward transformation." It is a public way of showing that one has repented of sins, has received God's forgiveness, has turned one's life over to Christ, and is prepared to walk in the resurrection of a new life in Christ. Baptism, for Mennonites, celebrates the gift of salvation, the gift of God's loving, forgiving, and enabling grace.

2. At the same time, this inner spiritual transformation within the heart of the individual is not sufficient in and of itself. For Mennonites, the act of baptizing with water is always a public event, done in the presence of the gathered congregation as a means of formally integrating the believer as a new member into the community of faith. Thus, Mennonite baptismal candidates not only confess their faith in Christ; they also promise to place themselves in the "care, discipline, and fellowship of the community." They commit themselves to give and receive counsel, to extend mutual aid, and to serve in the broader mission of the church. A faith that is purely private or subjective is incomprehensible within the Anabaptist-Mennonite tradition.

Like the doctrine of the incarnation, the baptism of water points toward a concrete, tangible expression of the invisible reality of the Spirit. It anchors the spiritual reality within the material world so that, in the words of the early Anabaptist leader Pilgram Marpeck, each becomes "a co-witness" of the other. Thus, even though Mennonites describe baptism as a symbol, it is never "merely" a symbol or "just" water. In a real sense, the public act of water baptism and the incorporation of the believer into the community evokes, or makes tangible, the movement of the Spirit.

3. Finally, the baptism of the Spirit and of water are closely related to the third strand of the baptismal cord in the Anabaptist-

Mennonite tradition: the baptism of blood. In its most literal form, the sixteenth-century Anabaptists understood the baptism of blood as a reminder to the new believer that following Christ in life meant being prepared to follow him in death as well. Throughout his ministry, Jesus seems to have a clear sense that the path he is traveling to Jerusalem will end in suffering. All along the way, he repeatedly warns his disciples that they must be prepared to give up power, to let go of their authority, and to loosen their grip on their own self-interest if they are to be part of the new kingdom that he is proclaiming.

Over and over again, the disciples fail to understand what Jesus is trying to tell them. At one point, when James and John argue with each other over who will sit at Jesus's right hand, Jesus asks them in a burst of frustration: "Can you drink the cup I drink and be baptized with the baptism I am baptized with?" (Mark 10:38). For the Anabaptists, the seriousness of the call to follow after Jesus was unmistakably clear in their baptismal vows. For many, baptism literally meant the possibility of persecution, torture, and death.

Although Mennonites in North America today are less likely to stress the baptism of blood in a literal sense, brothers and sisters in many other parts of the world (Colombia, Congo, Indonesia, and Vietnam, to name only a few) continue to face the reality of persecution. For them, as with the Anabaptists of the sixteenth century, the potential costs of their faith are a daily reminder that the decision to follow Christ is not a casual commitment. In the absence of direct persecution, Mennonites in North America are inclined to describe the baptism of blood in terms of an ongoing, active, and sometimes painful struggle of the Christian to die to the self and to follow after Jesus in daily life.

In either case, baptism in a Mennonite context not only symbolizes an inward change of heart and membership in the community of faith, but also a readiness to live out one's beliefs in tangible, concrete ways. Christian discipleship is a life of meaning, purpose, and joy. But it is also a process of submission, confession, and further repentance that inevitably involves inner struggle and suffering.

Baptism is therefore a public commitment to follow in the path of Jesus—a road that leads through death into the joy of the resurrection and new life.

Mennonite Understandings of the Atonement

This distinctive understanding of baptism is closely related to the way Mennonites think about the larger question of why Jesus came into the world. When Christians talk about salvation, they frequently describe Jesus as absolutely central to that process. Thus, we "accept Jesus into our heart as our Lord and personal Savior," or we say things such as "I have been saved by the blood of Jesus," or we sing songs about being "washed in his blood" (cf. Rev 7:14). Children who have grown up in Christian settings and heard these phrases or variations on them nearly every Sunday are likely to regard them as natural and normal. But for many teenagers, and especially for people like my Japanese friend who are not familiar with the Christian faith, these phrases can sound strange indeed. What exactly do we mean when we ask others to "invite Jesus into their heart"? How exactly does the blood of Jesus "poured out" for us "cleanse us from all our sins"?

At the heart of these questions is a theological concept that Christians call the atonement (literally, "at-one-ment"). Atonement refers to the means by which fallen, sinful human beings are restored to a relationship of intimacy and trust with God. It is how we are "made one" with God.

From the beginning of the church as it is described in the book of Acts and the letters that follow, Christians have tried to find appropriate language for describing the mission and the work of Christ. Since no human being can fully comprehend the nature of God, our language about God is inevitable metaphorical. That is, Christians always describe God as being like something else: a shepherd, a king, a mighty wind, and so on. The New Testament church, and theologians ever since, has also used metaphorical language to describe what God intended by sending Jesus into the world.

The dominant metaphor for the atonement in the New Testament is one that combines the language of ritual sacrifice from the Hebrew tradition with legal images of the courtroom drawn from first-century Rome. According to this view—sometimes called the satisfaction theory of atonement—the death of Jesus was necessary to satisfy God's honor and God's sense of justice.

Because human beings have all violated God's law, we deserve to be punished. God, who is righteous and just, demands satisfaction or atonement for the wrongs we have done. We human beings, however, are utterly incapable of ever atoning for our sins. Thus, Jesus accepted punishment in our place, thereby satisfying the divine requirement that sin be punished. Because Jesus was completely without sin, his innocent death "covers" the debt owed by all of humanity.

In many New Testament texts, this legal language of punishment and satisfaction is overlaid with the Hebrew image of ritual sacrifice. Here, just as a completely innocent lamb is sacrificed on behalf of the sins of a group, Jesus became a sacrificial lamb who suffered and died to appease the wrath of God, who demands justice for sins of humanity. In the Hebrew tradition, the shedding of blood is an important part of this sacrificial ritual. Out of this context the Christian tradition has adopted the language of "being washed in the blood of the Lamb."

There is much to be said in favor of this understanding of atonement. It conforms to our notion of justice, while preserving a sense of God's holiness and purity. It underscores the biblical theme of salvation offered to us as a free gift. And it describes Christ's suffering and death in a way that is supported by many New Testament texts. For all of these reasons Mennonites, along with the broader Christian tradition, have generally adopted this language of atonement.

At the same time, however, Mennonites also recognize that this is not the *only* way of describing the life and mission of Jesus. Just as baptism must be understood as having more than one meaning, so too, understandings of the atonement go beyond just the language of legal satisfaction or ritual sacrifice to describe the redemptive work of Jesus Christ.

Thus, for example, the Gospel of John describes Christ in terms of the Word (Logos)—identifying the Word as a bridge between God and humanity in a way that invites all who believe in Jesus to become part of the family of God (John 1:1-14). In Colossians, the resurrection emerges as a much more central theme in Jesus's mission on earth. Here Paul proclaims Jesus to be Lord over the principalities and powers, which have been "disarmed" by Christ's victory over the powers of death (Col 2:15). The letter to the Philippians describes Jesus as the new Adam, who freely accepted his humanity and did not consider equality with God as something to be grasped (Phil 2:5-11). In the example of Christ "emptying himself," taking on the role of a servant, we discover the paradox of a power "made perfect in weakness" (2 Cor 12:9). All of these images exist in the New Testament alongside that of Jesus's blood sacrifice on the cross.

The point is important for Mennonites because many Christians focus so much on the suffering and death of Christ that they virtually ignore the three years of Christ's work of teaching and healing. This is the reason why some Mennonites have expressed reservations about the Apostles' Creed: it moves directly from Christ's birth to his death, without any mention of his life. For some Christians, the consequence of this is to passively "claim the blood of Jesus" for our salvation and assume that nothing else in our lives needs to change. If this is the *only* Jesus that we preach and sing about—if we celebrate Jesus only as the sacrificial Lamb who died on our behalf so that the wrath of an angry God could be appeased—then we can easily become bystanders rather than participants in the adventure of Christian faith.

By the same token some Christians have so emphasized the wrath of God in Jesus's crucifixion that our image of God becomes distorted. Some have seen God as vindictive and vengeful, even using the language of God's demand for justice to support Christian acts of violence against nonbelievers. Here, too,

Mennonites want to exercise prudent caution.

Acknowledging that all our language about God is limited does not suggest a weak view of the atonement. Rather, it prompts us toward a continued posture of humility and gentleness in our witness to the truth.

Mennonite Understandings of Baptism: A Summary

As the multilayered meanings of baptism suggest, baptism in the Mennonite tradition is neither the beginning nor the end of the Christian journey. Like a wedding, baptism is a public statement of commitment offered before God and other witnesses reflecting a relationship that has existed long before the decision to make a formal and public vow. Like a wedding, it is an announcement of allegiances ("forsaking all others") clarifying that this relationship is now taking on a concrete and permanent character.

But just as the wedding is not yet a marriage, so too baptism should not be confused with what it means to be a Christian. The wedding defines some crucial understandings for the marriage ahead, but the real adventure of marriage is learning how to make a life together. Marriage is what it means to grow in the relationship, to establish a home, to raise a family, to adjust to inevitable changes and unexpected challenges, and to practice daily the virtues of love, compassion, trust, forgiveness, and fidelity.

Mennonites understand baptism in much the same way. It is an event of utmost importance that gives public witness to our allegiances and celebrates God's transforming work in our lives. Yet baptism is really only a point of reference for the real adventure of Christian discipleship. Like a wedding, it is not the culmination of a relationship but a moment of conscious commitment that points ahead to a lifetime relationship with God and with fellow believers. This relationship is filled with further opportunities for confession and repentance, adjusting to surprising changes, and deepening in love as the mystery of intimacy and the joy of relationship are renewed every day.

6

Believers Baptism

A Critique... and Ongoing Questions

During the course of the sixteenth century, the practice of believers baptism sparked a sharply negative reaction from church and civil authorities that eventually led to the public execution of some three thousand Anabaptists. Today, of course, the separation of church and state and the freedom of religion are now cornerstones in the American democratic system. But for many people in the sixteenth century, the theological and political implications of a free church were deeply troubling. In making faith a matter of individual choice, the Anabaptists seemed not only to imperil the soul of the infant but also to undermine the very basis of a Christian social and political order. Thankfully, no one today is advocating the death penalty for churches that practice believers baptism. But many of the same questions remain.

1. Will Unbaptized Babies Go to Hell? As we have seen, most Catholics and many Protestants believed that human beings, since the Fall of Adam and Eve, are born with a sinful character. Hence, they are destined to damnation even before they are consciously aware of their choices. "In Adam's fall, we sinned all," claimed the medieval couplet. To be sure, some traditions have developed slightly more nuanced understandings of this principle, largely out of pastoral concerns for the parents of stillborn infants or babies that die before the benefit of baptism. But the general principle of infant baptism in Catholic and Protestant traditions is shaped by the awareness of original sin and the complete, utter dependence of the human on God and the church for faith. The ritual of baptism confers a mark of God's blessing that saves the infant from the damnation of hell. It incorporates the baby into a body of believers whose faith will "stand in" for the child until they are ready to claim it for themselves.

Mennonites are not naively optimistic about human nature; but they do take issue with the notion that infants are damned to hell from the moment of their birth. To the contrary, in the Gospels Jesus consistently suggests that children are in a state of innocence. He even points to them as models for how adults ought to act: trusting, simple, and vulnerable. "Unless you change and become like little children," Jesus told his disciples, "you will never enter the kingdom of heaven" (Matt 18:3). So Mennonites begin with an assumption that children are born in innocence. At some point, however, children begin to lose their spiritual innocence. They start to make conscious choices against God's desire for them. At some point—what some Mennonites call the "age of accountability"—every person needs to make a decision about their basic orientation in life—whether it will be directed toward God or toward the self.

2. Voluntary Baptism Imposes a Division Within Christian Society, Suggesting That Not Everyone Is Truly a Christian. For the vast majority of people who had been born and raised in the Catholic church, the Anabaptist insistence on voluntary baptism suggested that their baptisms as infants were of no spiritual significance. Such a view seemed arrogant and presumptuous. It seemed to separate the true church, made up of a handful of adult baptized believers, from the rest of society.

Though this concern is understandable, from a Mennonite perspective it is only partially true. To be sure, Mennonites would insist that Christian identity is not a birthright, conferred by the ritual of baptism that automatically follows the birth of a child into a Christian family. Because the decision to follow Jesus has real consequences, it must be a conscious choice made by every individual. And because the church is not the same thing as the state or society in general, Mennonites do not assume that everyone born in a Christian territory is automatically a Christian.

At the same time, however, Mennonites are cautious about making judgments regarding the salvation of other Christians. If people claim to be Christians, few Mennonites would presume to play the role of God and make pronouncements regarding their future status in heaven or hell, even if their understanding of faith is quite different from Mennonite teachings. Although Mennonites take the call to discernment seriously, they do not readily assume the responsibility of final judgment.

3. By Linking Salvation to Human Choice, Voluntary Baptism Undermines the Reality of Grace as a Free Gift. Perhaps the most problematic aspect of Mennonite baptism, especially for contemporary Protestants, is a foundational theological issue regarding the nature of salvation itself. Luther and the mainline Protestant reformers emphatically rejected the idea that humans were capable of "earning" their salvation through good deeds: human are saved by Christ's sacrificial death and by God's initiative of grace and election alone. No human attitude or action could possibly merit God's free gift of grace. This was a simple point, but it was the hinge upon which almost all of Protestant theology turned. Humans cannot contribute anything to their salvation.

The point might seem obvious if you focus primarily on the standard list of good deeds and moral behavior. Most Mennonites would readily acknowledge that we are never as virtuous as we could or should be. Indeed, even our most virtuous actions are often tainted by the hope of public recognition or receiving something in return. But the deeper issue is actually more subtle and complicated than this. In the theology of Luther and Calvin, our most basic desires are thoroughly corrupted, including the will.

Human beings cannot even *choose* to accept God's grace. In fact, linking salvation with human choice, they argued, leads us back into the illusion that we can somehow contribute something to our salvation. This was the problem they saw in believers baptism. When Mennonites insist that the decision to accept Christ's gift of grace is a conscious choice, it implies that the believer is somehow participating in the act of salvation. It appears to open the door to a false theology of works righteousness based on human initiative.

From a Mennonite perspective a legitimate concern is raised here. Most Mennonites would share the Protestant affirmation of grace and reject a view of Christianity that is based on good works or the notion that humans can somehow earn or merit their salvation by virtuous living. Baptism, after all, is an outward sign of an *inward* transformation—and that inward transformation is all God's doing. We are transformed by God's grace, not by our actions.

But at the same time, Mennonites respond, we are not robots. Human beings do not simply act out God's script in a passive or mechanical way, like marionettes on a string. If that were the case, why would there be so much emphasis in the New Testament on following after Jesus? Why would there be a concern about judgment? Why would Christians offer prayers of supplication? Or why would Jesus say, "If you forgive men when they sin against you, your heavenly Father will also forgive you" (Matt 6:14), suggesting that the choices human beings make are indeed linked in a meaningful way to God's response?

Clearly, grace comes from God as a gift: there is nothing that we can do to earn God's forgiveness. But gifts must be accepted. Somebody can offer you an all-expenses-paid twelve-day vacation to the Caribbean islands, but the gift only has real meaning for you if you choose to actually go on the trip. Alternately, to extend the metaphor, you can take a week-old baby on such a vacation, but the baby will have no recollection of the event and no frame of reference to appreciate its significance. The Mennonite practice of believers baptism recognizes that humans are free to accept or reject God's gift of grace. Jesus consistently assumed that the person being baptized was capable of belief and instruction. Baptism in the Gospels is clearly linked to a response to an invitation to follow Jesus.

Ongoing Questions for Mennonites

1. What Is the Appropriate Age of Baptism? Mennonites have not generally established any fixed principles regarding the proper age of baptism, granting congregations and individuals a wide degree of freedom in determining the appropriate moment. The biblical texts are not especially clear in this matter. The story of Jesus's youthful encounter with the Jewish teachers in Jerusalem, has suggested to some people that the age of twelve is a useful benchmark for the age of accountability. Yet anyone who has been to a junior youth event knows that the maturity level of twelve-year-olds can vary widely. Others, trying to preserve a clear sense of the voluntary nature of baptism, have suggested that no one should be baptized until they have left home and are able to make that decision free from the direct influence of their parents. After all, they note, Jesus himself was not baptized until sometime around the age of thirty.

In practice, the question is generally resolved on an individual and congregational basis. And the resolution of the question almost always reflects an implicit bias favoring one particular strand in the meaning of baptism over another. Thus, for example, if the parents or a congregation regard baptism primarily as a sign of repentance and forgiveness (baptism of the Spirit), prompted by a recognition of our sinful nature, then it may be appropriate to baptize children at a young age, perhaps even ages five to eight. If, however, the emphasis is primarily on incorporation into the local congregation (symbolized by the baptism of water), with a commitment to give and receive counsel or accept leadership roles, then a somewhat older age is probably more fitting—perhaps an age more in line with broader social responsibilities such as receiving a driver's license or voting. Similarly, if you look at baptism primarily as a commitment to Christian obedience, even unto death (baptism of blood), then the appropriate age is likely much closer to adulthood. On the whole, Mennonites have traditionally not baptized children under the age of ten or so, but they have not made firm statements on this. They recognize it as a matter for local discernment among the child, parents, leadership, and the broader congregation.

2. Is Choice Different Than Socialization? The question of the appropriate age of baptism is closely related to another concern sometimes raised within Mennonite congregations. How do we preserve a sense of a genuine choice when young people are often socialized into the faith by their upbringing in a Mennonite home, a Mennonite congregation, and possibly even a Mennonite school? Raised in tight-knit communities, surrounded by other Mennonites, how is it possible to talk meaningfully about choice when everything in the culture is tipped toward compliance?

These are important questions, especially since some congregations have fallen into a practice of routinely baptizing everyone in the eighth-grade class or at the time of their sixteenth birthday. But a larger perspective would need to recognize that we never make any decisions, least of all decisions about basic directions in life, in a vacuum. In a media-saturated culture, with powerful voices championing a materialistic, individualistic, and purely secular worldview, it is clear that a decision *not* to follow Jesus is never made in a value-neutral context. On the contrary, we are constantly making choices within settings that shape those decisions in complex ways.

For Mennonites, it is crucial that this context not be coercive. But it would be naive to suggest that Mennonite parents are indifferent to the outcome of their children's choices. There is no virtue in raising children as if the decision to follow Jesus is simply one more consumer choice in the marketplace of lifestyle options—on the same level, say, as joining a health club. The mandate for Christian missions involves appropriate sensitivity to developmental stages, to be sure, but without apology for sharing the good news.

3. What About Infant-Parent Dedication? The Mennonite practice of publicly dedicating a newborn child goes back to the sixteenth century, although North American Mennonites have revived the practice only within the past fifty years or so. Despite some parallels, infant dedication should not be confused with infant baptism. The Mennonite service is a public recognition that the birth of a child is a gift from God and worthy of celebration. Dedicating a child to God is an expression of thanks for the gift of new life—innocent, precious—that serves as a sign of hope and joy.

Although the congregation is indeed dedicating the infant to God, at a deeper level the service is really a public dedication of the parents and the congregation to the spiritual care and nurture of the child. By committing themselves to participate in the child's spiritual upbringing, the congregation is not embarking on a path of indoctrination or brainwashing. But as every parent knows, raising children is an all-consuming task, one that ideally involves the assistance of the entire community. The nurture and discipline offered by a loving community makes God's invitation to faith tangible—pointing the way to a life of joy.

4. Is Baptism Always into a Specific Congregation or into the Broader Christian church? Since baptism for Mennonites is strongly associated with membership in a local congregation, there is little precedent in the Anabaptist-Mennonite tradition for baptizing new converts generically as Christians. From a Mennonite perspective, baptism apart from an identity with a local congregation suggests either that the very act of baptism saves a person—that baptism is a sacrament conferring salvation—or that baptism is a private act devoid of any public significance or congregational accountability. Both of these alternatives seem unacceptable.

At the same time, arguments in favor of generic baptisms should not be simply dismissed out of hand. After all, some people have argued, Philip baptized the Ethiopian eunuch, apparently in private and without any clear accountability to a local congregation (Acts 8:38). And the household baptisms mentioned elsewhere in the book of Acts do not give prominent emphasis to congregational involvements.

Nonetheless, in the great commission Jesus makes it clear that baptism is closely linked to instruction ("teaching them to observe all things"); and nothing in Scripture suggests that the Christian life is that of a free-floating individualist. A Mennonite understanding of the New Testament frames the Christian walk clearly within a context of other believers. We come to know Christ, we mature in our faith, and we deepen in our understanding of God's will and purpose for the world through our fellowship within the gathered body of believers.

As we will see in a later chapter, Mennonites do recognize that the church is bigger than just their denomination. With other Christians around the world, we share in the universal message of love, forgiveness, and discipleship that comes as a gift from the Holy Spirit. So baptism, like faith, always has a universal as well as a particular meaning to it. But at the same time, we cannot fully understand or express this universal truth apart from concrete, particular, local, day-to-day interactions with other believers.

For these reasons, Mennonites clearly associate baptism with membership into a congregation. If a person moves to a new community, the home church customarily sends a "letter of transfer" to their new congregation, attesting to the individual's faith, identifying specific gifts, and encouraging the process of incorporation into the new church. None of this is intended to be coercive or controlling. The Mennonite church is a free and voluntary association. But it does express a deep awareness that, in baptism, we have committed ourselves to a particular group of people. It gives tangible expression to the interdependent nature of faith. We are not Christians in isolation from each other. Indeed, many newcomers regard the high value placed on congregational participation as an attractive feature of the Mennonite church, something to be celebrated amid the self-centered loneliness so pervasive in modern culture.

5. What Is the Appropriate Form or Mode of Baptism? Agreeing on the correct procedure for the ritual of baptism has often been a source of tension in the Christian tradition. Mennonites have not been immune to controversy on this point. The practice of immersion—whether in a stream, a pond, or a baptismal font—has traditionally been understood to replicate the pattern of Jesus's own baptism. Immersion carries with it a strong symbolic sense of the death and resurrection of Christ pointing toward a new birth. So some Mennonite congregations have preferred this practice. A few—notably the Mennonite Brethren—have insisted that immersion is the most appropriate form of biblical baptism.

Historians have speculated that the need for secrecy probably encouraged some early Christians to baptize in more private settings. This may have led to an alternative mode of baptism by pouring, in which the leader of the service pours or sprinkles water over the head of the kneeling candidate. Here the symbolism suggests the "pouring out" of the Holy Spirit at Pentecost (Acts 2). Early Anabaptist congregations seem to have followed this practice, also for reasons of secrecy. But in other examples Anabaptist groups met in secluded parts of the forest to hold baptisms outside, presumably by immersion.

Although some congregations have found themselves deeply divided over this question, most Mennonites today are quite flexible about the mode of baptism. Clearly, from a theological perspective the method of baptism is far less important than the broader set of meanings associated with the practice. Baptism involves a public commitment to faith in Christ, incorporation into the local congregation, and a vow to follow in the path of Jesus.

6. Do People Who Were Baptized as Infants in Other Denominations Need to Be Rebaptized If They Join a Mennonite Church? For most of Anabaptist-Mennonite history the answer to this question would have been an unequivocal "yes." After all, this question was at the core of Anabaptist identity in the sixteenth century. Precisely because the Anabaptists refused to baptize their babies, reserving this ritual instead for people old enough to confess their faith, they were imprisoned, tortured, and executed. If the person—in this case, the infant being baptized—did not *choose* that baptism, or if they could not remember their baptism, in what sense did it signify their public commitment to faith in Christ or a desire to follow in the way of Jesus? For these reasons, the Anabaptists strenuously resisted the label imposed on them of being "re-baptizers" since they understood the ritual undertaken at their birth not as a baptism but only as a meaningless sprinkling of water.

The arguments against the baptism of a new member who has been baptized as an infant are generally pastoral in nature: for some, the expectation of rebaptism seems to challenge the integrity of Christian life and practice of the new member. It suggests that the new member was not a Christian during the time that they were not part of the Mennonite church. What would baptism signify, some might ask, that has not already been made sufficiently evident in the quality of their Christian life before the baptism? In response to these concerns, a growing number of Mennonite congregations are considering this question on a case-by-case basis, or as a matter of local discernment. Some allow such individuals to join on confession of their faith (but without rebaptism) as a clear exception to the general principle, while others have been more explicit and inviting in making this a clear option.

In the end, this is probably not a point about which congregations are going to divide. In the Mennonite understanding, salvation does not ultimately hinge on the act of baptism. But congregations have good reasons to be thoughtful, and even cautious, about their rationale for changing their procedures in a practice as elemental to Mennonite identity as baptism. Newcomers who are attracted to Mennonite faith and practice should recognize that the community they are about to join has an identity that existed long before their participation with the group. Practices and beliefs can be challenged and altered, of course, but a community cannot sustain itself if its basic convictions are open for fundamental reformulation each time a newcomer joins. Since symbols give structure to community life and practice, they should not be casually disregarded or reformulated. Finally, given the centrality of believers baptism to the five-hundred-year history of the Anabaptist-

Mennonite tradition, one might legitimately ask whether newcomers fully understand the nature of the community they seek to join if they are strongly resistant to a practice constitutive of the group's very identity.

Nonbaptized believers who have long fellowshipped with Mennonites and are now ready to formally join a congregation might think of their baptism as something analogous to the naturalization ceremony that foreigners undergo when they become citizens of the United States. Many who participate in these ceremonies have lived in the country for a long time. They have been productive members of the community who have obeyed the law, paid their taxes, and participated fully in the local culture. To all outward appearances, they are citizens.

Yet, the naturalization ceremony marks a clear, public statement about the seriousness of their commitment; it makes formal what had hitherto only been assumed. And even though it seems as if nothing has changed in the basic character or attitude of the new citizen, the event carries with it a new set of privileges and responsibilities that do indeed have meaning. In a similar way, believers baptism fixes our commitments to God, the church, and daily discipleship in a moment of time that is accessible to public memory. It celebrates and anchors a pattern of life already long in formation.

Summary

Voluntary baptism, or believers baptism—and the rich array of meanings and associations woven into the event—is clearly central to Mennonite faith and life. For biblical and theological reasons, it is a core conviction that distinguishes Mennonites in some important ways from the Catholic tradition and from many Protestant denominations. At the same time, however, not every question surrounding baptism has been resolved within the Mennonite church; so despite the importance of the practice, there is still room for congregational discernment and open conversation on the subject.

The context of that discussion has changed dramatically since the sixteenth century. For the Anabaptists, believers baptism was a deeply divisive symbol that seemed to undermine established church practice and to threaten the social and political order of the day, even to the point where the practice became a capital offense. Today, by contrast, the principle of individual liberty in matters of conscience is so firmly entrenched in American public life that the Mennonite understanding of believers baptism seems far less radical. This is good news for Mennonites in that it means they are no longer persecuted for refusing to baptize infants. But the danger is that baptism can become merely a symbol, or worse, an automatic rite of passage that is more of a social recognition of adolescent coming of age than a spiritual reality marking the transformation of soul and character.

On this issue significant theological differences separate Mennonites from many other Christian groups. At the same time, in the context of a postmodern, highly secularized culture, all denominations have become "free churches" in the sense that the public culture can no longer be counted on to uphold or embrace Christian values. Hence, churches of every sort are becoming much more deliberate and self-conscious about the nature of Christian commitment in nurturing new Christians in faith and incorporating them into the life of the church.

7

Faith as Discipleship

Christian Practices in the Mennonite Tradition 1

Few stories from the New Testament are more simple—and at the same time, more profound—than the account of Jesus calling the first disciples. One day early in his ministry, Jesus encounters Peter, Andrew, James, and John casting their nets in the Sea of Galilee. We know virtually nothing about these men other than the fact that they are hardworking, presumably uneducated, fishermen. Yet when Jesus asks them to drop their nets and to follow him, "immediately they left" (Matt 4:22). And with that decision, their lives are forever changed.

We have the advantage, of course, of knowing how this story unfolds. The Gospels tell the account of the disciples' journey with Jesus: their wonder at his miracles, their struggle to understand his parables; and their commitment and waverings through the events leading up to the crucifixion; the resurrection; then the dramatic story of the early church in Acts. But for Peter, Andrew, James, and John, the decision to follow Jesus is a step of faith into the unknown.

The disciples soon discover that following Jesus transforms their lives. To be sure, they still live in the same country, speak the same language, and are part of the same culture as before. Now, however, they see the familiar landscape from the perspective of the Messiah, as they struggle to understand what it means to follow a Master who insists that "the first will be last" (Mark 10:31) and that being great means being "the servant of all" (9:35).

When Mennonites talk about what it means to be a Christian, the word they are most likely to use is discipleship. The characteristics they are most likely to associate with discipleship are themes of service and love. The story is sometimes told of a Mennonite farmer who encounters a traveling preacher. When the preacher asks him if he is saved, the farmer responds: "I could tell you anything you want to hear. If you really want to know if I am a Christian, you will need to ask my neighbors."

Although Mennonites can sometimes sound as though they are trapped in a religion of works, the deeper reality is that they are skeptical about a faith that consists mostly of words, feelings, or ceremonies. When we are baptized, we are choosing to follow after Jesus—to drop our nets, to let go of the assumptions of the culture around us, and to become disciples in a risky, joyous journey of faith. This is not always easy. And Mennonites, like the disciples, are often slow to understand fully what Jesus is saying. But our orientation—historically and theologically—is to be ready to break with the conventional wisdom of the culture around us and to follow Jesus, even though the path is filled with uncertainties and risks.

The Radical Teachings of Jesus

Throughout the centuries Christians have always struggled to know how to interpret the teachings of Jesus, especially the more radical instructions that seem to fly in the face of common sense and all of our natural instincts. "Love your enemies and pray for those who persecute you," Jesus tells a crowd gathered on a hillside (Matt 5:44). "Sell everything you have . . . then come, follow me," he instructs the rich young ruler (Luke 18:22). "You will never enter the kingdom of heaven," he tells his bewildered disciples, "unless you change and become like little children" (Matt 18:3). And to Nicodemus he says, "You must be born again" (John 3:3).

Many Christians have assumed that ordinary people cannot be expected to take this dramatic language of conversion or these radical teachings too literally. We can take comfort in the promise of salvation already received in our infant baptism, the argument goes, and we should try our best to be virtuous and charitable. But the high standards of Christ are too much to expect of normal Christians living amid the messy realities of daily life.

Still, the teachings of Jesus do not go away. The Catholic church resolved this tension by creating a special category of Christians—monks and nuns—who were willing to devote themselves completely to the high standards of Christ. People in monastic orders were committed to lives of prayer, simplicity, chastity, economic sharing, nonviolence, hospitality to the poor, and care of the sick—in short, to live as close as possible to the concrete teachings of Jesus. So the church did not simply dismiss the standard, or give up on it altogether. Instead, discipleship became an option for a small group of special Christians who had a unique calling to this radical way of life.

The Protestant reformers, by contrast, rejected the monastic option. In fact, they reserved special criticism for monks and nuns and regarded the whole monastic system as based on a flawed understanding of salvation. Pilgrimages, rituals of confession and penance, and especially the monastic life of rigorous discipline, they argued, made God's free gift of grace dependent on pious deeds. This was a perversion of the gospel since, as Luther tirelessly repeated, we are saved by grace, not by our works.

To be sure, the reformers did not reject Jesus's teachings out of hand. But they tended to shift the primary focus of his mission from Teacher or Example to a more spiritual role as Savior. Salvation, they insisted, depends solely on Christ's sacrificial blood poured out on the cross. This was his real mission and purpose for coming to the world. The teachings of Jesus, at best, make it clear that we are fundamentally unable to do what he taught, so that, condemned by our consistent inability to carry out the law, we find ourselves falling back into the arms of grace.

Mennonites owe a significant theological debt to both Catholics and Protestants, but they differ in several important ways on the question of discipleship or ethics. With their Catholic neighbors, Mennonites share a conviction that faith calls the Christian to concrete acts of obedience and to the high standard of Jesus represented in the monastic orders. But Mennonites are not ready to say that this is a standard intended only for the spiritual elite. Instead, Mennonites believe that the difficult sayings of Jesus—his teachings in the Sermon on the Mount, for example, about loving enemies—are meant to be followed by all Christians, not just a few heroic exceptions. Likewise, along with many of their Protestant neighbors, Mennonites believe that we are saved by God's gift of grace. But they are not ready to regard faith only as a spiritual transaction by which the divine grace of God cancels our sin. True faith, they believe, will inevitably find concrete expression in a changed, transformed way of life. Or as the book of James says, "Faith without works is dead" (2:20, 26, KJV).

A Radical Reorientation: "On Earth as It Is in Heaven"

In the prayer that he taught his followers, Jesus offers an insight into the nature of Christian discipleship. The Lord's Prayer (Matt 6:9-13)—repeated every Sunday by millions of Christians around the world—begins, appropriately, by giving honor to God: "Hallowed be your name." Then it describes just what praise and honor to God actually look like. God is honored when his kingdom comes and his will is done "on earth as it is in heaven." Many Christians have repeated these words so often that they no longer really hear what they are praying. When we ask that God's will be done "on earth as it is in heaven," we are anticipating that life on earth as we know and experience it is going to be transformed in the light of God's will and purposes. "From now on," writes Paul, "we regard no one from a human point of view. . . . If anyone is in

Christ, there is a *new creation:* everything old has passed away; see, everything has become new!" (2 Cor 5:16-17, NRSV). To become a disciple of Christ means that we look at the world from a new perspective. All of the most basic assumptions of human experience that we accept as "natural" are part of the creation that is now being renewed in Christ.

According to the account in Genesis (1-3), the world that God created and called "good" has been poisoned by sin and is badly in need of redemption. The poison of sin is much more pervasive than just an isolated act or the occasional evildoer disrupting orderly society. Like a drop of arsenic in a well, sin has tainted all of creation. And the consequences of sin in our world are evident everywhere one looks: the wars of nations; the violence in our homes; the grinding reality of poverty; the costly seduction of addictions; even the well-intended social program that diminishes the spirit as it feeds the body. The list could go on and on.

For Mennonites, Christian discipleship offers a radical alternative to the pervasive reality of a sinful creation. For them, following Jesus is not primarily a private spiritual transaction (to accept Jesus in my heart), an emotion-filled charismatic experience, or the practice of taking communion on a regular basis—valuable though all of these may be. Rather, following Jesus is a commitment to participate in God's transforming, redemptive work in the world, bearing witness to a "new creation" made possible by Christ, so that God's will is indeed made evident "on earth as it is in heaven."

At the heart of this new creation is a surprising and paradoxical understanding of power. It is not that disciples of Jesus are powerless—far from it. When sending out the seventy-two apostles to proclaim the good news of the kingdom, Jesus says, "I have given you authority to trample on snakes and scorpions and to overcome all the power of the enemy; nothing will harm you" (Luke 10:19). But the power that Jesus lived and taught was the paradoxical power of human vulnerability, in which human weakness allowed the presence of God to be fully revealed.

Over and over in the Gospels, Jesus tries to communicate to his disciples that the kingdom he is introducing operates by different principles than those of the kingdoms of the world. In his kingdom, Jesus tells them, "the first will be last." In his kingdom, those who are meek, merciful, and gentle are the ones who will receive a blessing. In his kingdom, love and compassion are more powerful than the coercive force of violence and the threat of physical pain or death. Indeed, it is only by being a servant, by emptying oneself, that the glory and power of God can be revealed and God's will be truly done "on earth as it is in heaven."

So discipleship begins with a commitment to accept Jesus's call to follow him. It offers a visible witness to a new order of creation that God is bringing about within a fallen world. And it finds expression in tangible acts of love and service.

Before describing some more specific forms that discipleship has taken within the Mennonite tradition, it is important to clarify two crucial points frequently misunderstood. First, discipleship is not primarily a set of rules that must be obeyed. A Mennonite understanding of faith, as we have seen, is always embodied; faith always finds expression in the world of flesh and blood. But sometimes Mennonites have allowed this commitment to faith-in-action to collapse into heavy-handed legalism.

The response to legalism is a regular reminder that the Lord's Prayer begins by orienting us properly in relationship to God. Our chief aim, helpfully declares the Westminster Catechism (used especially in the Reformed tradition), "is to glorify God, and fully to enjoy him forever." Discipleship therefore, is always to be understood as an expression of thanksgiving and glory to God; it is our response to God's transforming love.

A second crucial point, to be developed in more detail in the following chapter, is that discipleship is not for loners or individual heroes: Christian discipleship cannot be pursued alone. The context for the new creation that Paul writes about is always within a community of believers. We become the people God wants us to be by practicing discipleship together.

The rest of the chapter offers an overview of a Mennonite

approach to discipleship structured around three basic aspects of human life: money, sex, and power. In each of these areas, Mennonites have asked how their commitment to Christ changes their understanding of these fundamental human realities, and how these natural impulses might be redeemed and transformed in the direction of the new creation.

Money: A Commitment to Stewardship, Simplicity, and Generosity

In the spring of 1989, the wheels of world history took a sudden and unexpected turn. Following a series of rapid political and economic reforms that nobody could have fully foreseen, the East German government opened its borders and, for the first time in nearly thirty years, permitted its citizens to travel freely outside the country. Live images of people dancing with joy on top of the infamous Berlin Wall, followed by scenes of the wall's destruction, captured the euphoria of the event. For many, the collapse of the Berlin Wall marked the ultimate victory of democratic capitalism over a failed socialist system that was destructive to the creative spirit. Today, capitalist economies have proved to be highly productive—the motor driving the world marketplace and the hopes of a better life for all those who participate in the global economy.

It has been tempting for many Christians in North America to look on the triumph of capitalism in eastern Europe and around the world as divinely ordained. After all, capitalism is premised on a view of human nature that is deeply biblical. It values hard work and delayed gratification. It rewards discipline. And it recognizes the powerful drive of human innovation and creativity.

Yet, Christians should be cautious about confusing any economic system—socialist and capitalist alike—as part of God's new creation. For all of its many obvious benefits, capitalism still reflects the reality of a fallen world. Indeed, the engine behind the productivity in capitalist economies is the fact that humans are, by nature, competitive, selfish, and greedy. The alchemy of greed ultimately transforms the coarse ore of individual self-interest into the gold of market productivity. If everyone pursues private gain, the logic goes, the laws of supply and demand will guarantee that the broader public will benefit. In other words, greed is good! This observation, so basic to human experience, might explain the success of capitalism, but it is hardly a biblical concept.

Jesus said little about either capitalism or socialism, but he had a great deal to say about wealth and generosity. In his teachings the call to discipleship is an invitation to become a "new creature in Christ." This new creation takes precisely those aspects of human nature that capitalism thrives on—greed, selfishness, self-centeredness—and transforms them into compassion, generosity, and vulnerability.

When the market logic of our day pushes us to regard every aspect of life as a commodity, Jesus asks us to look beyond the material into the heart. When our current economic assumptions tend to reduce human beings into little more than producers and consumers, Jesus invites us to regard all people with the dignity and respect appropriate to beings created in the image of God. When advertisements feed us lies about the good life and trap us into illusions about what it means to be a whole person, Jesus offers us a truth that will truly set us free. When the logic of the world is to store up for ourselves treasures on earth, Jesus reminds us that our treasure is ultimately in heaven. "But seek first his kingdom and his righteousness, and all these things will be given to you as well" (Matt 6:33).

Taking discipleship seriously in the economic realm does not necessarily mean that Mennonites reject all aspects of business and commerce. Indeed, over the past fifty years or so, the number of Mennonite entrepreneurs, manufacturers, and retailers has increased enormously. All of us, in one way or another, participate in the complex interrelations of a consumer society and the global economy. Yet, at the same time, Mennonites generally stop short of giving an unequivocal blessing to the marketplace, always aware that the New Creation that God has in mind for his people is based on a different worldview than the logic of capitalism or socialism.

1. Christian Stewardship. Mennonites believe that *all* that we have—our time, our creative talents, our resources, the earth itself—comes to us as a gift from God. To be sure, we may have worked for our education, or had the insight to pursue a market opportunity, or invented a machine to increase productivity, or crafted an effective marketing strategy. But from a Christian perspective, we cannot claim to own any of this. All that we have comes to us as a loan from God and is only temporarily in our possession. The possessions we have are not to be grasped and hoarded, as if we controlled our own security and destiny. Rather, we have been entrusted with resources that ultimately belong to God. In a real and tangible sense, we are only caretakers or *stewards* of God's creation.

This view of stewardship suggests a principle much broader than the traditional Christian understanding of the tithe. Based on the Old Testament practice of contributing a tenth of one's produce each year to the temple, the tithe suggests that we voluntarily give up a certain percentage of our assets to the church or to God. Stewardship, by contrast, is a reminder that we are merely returning something that never did belong to us. Tithing tends to regard our offerings as a kind of tax assessment on our income. Stewardship calls us to the spiritual discipline of freeing ourselves from the very concept of ownership.

2. Work Is Good . . . So Is the Sabbath. Mennonites believe that hard work—the disciplined skill of the artisan and professional, the creative expressions of poets and musicians and artists, the routine tasks of the parent and farmer—is a reflection of God's original act of creation. Work that is honest and constructive, that heals and reconciles, that makes the world more beautiful—all such work celebrates the goodness of God.

Mennonites can be found in many different occupations: as managers and laborers, as white-collar and blue-collar workers, in service professions and agriculture. We honor the creative energy of productive work. But at the same time, Mennonites have traditionally also taken seriously the commandment to honor the principle of the Sabbath. In decades past some Mennonites even honored Sabbath rest to the point of legalism, establishing precise rules about what the Christian could or could not do on the Lord's Day (Sunday).

The deeper meaning of the Sabbath, however, is that God desires for us to have a structured way of maintaining an appropriate perspective on our labor. In setting aside the Sabbath for worship, we remind ourselves of the central themes of stewardship—that all of our possessions, talents, and desires belong to God. In resting on the Sabbath, and in being attentive to our Sabbath activities, we bear witness to the culture around us that we are more than merely producers and consumers. Not shopping on the Sabbath, for example, is a profound statement in our market-obsessed society that we can control our hunger to consume. Not working on the Sabbath is a declaration that humans are more than just machines, generating output.

Today, Mennonites are apt to be far less restrictive about their Sabbath activities than they might have been fifty years ago. But the principle at stake here is a serious one. By observing the Sabbath, disciples of Jesus remember *who* they are and *whose* they are. In meaningful labor we participate in making the world a better place; in meaningful rest we glorify God and remember that we are first and foremost children of God.

3. An Appreciation for Simplicity and Functionality. In comparison with our brothers and sisters in the Southern Hemisphere, Mennonites in North America can only be described as wealthy. But even though we have benefited enormously from our participation in a productive economy, we also show signs of suffering spiritually from the materialism, consumerism, and frantic busyness of the culture in which we live. As an antidote to the pervasive worship of affluence, many Mennonites have tried to cultivate a conscious lifestyle of simplicity based on the life and teachings of Jesus. "See how the lilies of the field grow," Jesus teaches. "They do not labor or spin. Yet I tell you that not even Solomon in all his splendor was dressed like one of these" (Matt 6:28-29). In the same passage Jesus also admonishes his disciples to simplicity in speech: "Simply let your 'Yes' be 'Yes,' and your 'No,' 'No'" (5:37).

Mennonites have sometimes allowed these teachings on simplicity to lead to an aesthetic of austerity or to an almost legalistic embrace of simple living and recycling. At its best, however, the Mennonite impulse toward simplicity is an affirmation of the freedom of the Christian. It is a rejection of the compulsive tendency to prop up our identity by accumulating more things, and it recognizes that the pressure to "keep up with the Joneses" holds us hostage to an illusion. It is no accident that one of the all-time best-selling Mennonite volumes is the *More-with-Less Cookbook,* which celebrates the simplicity of good food shared in the company of others. Extensive experience by many Mennonites as development workers in poorer countries has also fostered an appreciation for a simpler lifestyle that consumes fewer limited resources and fosters a greater sense of dependency on each other and on God.

4. We Are Interconnected. There is a powerful impulse in our society, and especially within the market forces of our economy, to think and act in ways that benefit us as individuals. Even if we rarely state it so baldly, our natural inclinations are toward the survival of the fittest, with all of us inclined to seek a competitive advantage over those around us. By focusing first and foremost on ourselves, we often tend to make decisions that ignore the weaker members of society—the sick, the uneducated, the immigrant, the elderly, the poor—or to overlook the long-term environmental consequences that our economic decisions might have for the generations that will follow us.

Discipleship in the Mennonite tradition calls us to look beyond ourselves in our economic practices. Disciples of Jesus honor the image of God that resides in all people. They recognize the inherent dignity of every person, especially those who find themselves at the margins of respectability. We don't live unto ourselves in the new creation. "I tell you the truth, whatever you did for one of the least of these brothers of mine, you did for me" (Matt 25:40).

Not only are we connected through Christ with the people around us; we are also connected to the earth: to the soil, water, and air that God has entrusted to us in stewardship. Destroying God's creation for private gain or bequeathing environmental problems to later generations to resolve is blatantly selfish. Such an attitude reflects the fallenness of the world which disciples of Christ are called to redeem.

Respect for the environment does not mean that Christians worship the earth or that we can somehow live without leaving any trace of our presence in the natural world. Rather, Christian stewardship and love for others simply compel us to be attentive to how we treat God's created world.

5. A Spirit of Generosity. Christians have long debated about what Jesus meant when he said, "Give to the one who asks" (Matt 5:42), or "It is easier for a camel to go through the eye of a needle than for a rich man to enter the kingdom of God" (19:24). Some have insisted that he was speaking metaphorically or that his words were meant only for listeners in first-century Palestine. Others have seen in these teachings a call to voluntary poverty as an expression of our complete trust in God. Mennonites are not of one mind about how to interpret these passages. But they are at least agreed that Christians ultimately should place their trust in God rather than in their possessions. In the world we often give up our possessions grudgingly—either out of a sense of guilty obligation to charity or in a barely disguised form of coercion when the Internal Revenue Service redistributes wealth through the tax system. By contrast, disciples following in the path of Christ are called to give lavishly of their possessions—and to do so with a cheerful heart and in the same spirit of reckless generosity that we have received from God.

Here again, the principle of generosity suggests an attitude of freedom more than it does a list of precise rules about how much we ought to give or how much we hold on to. True generosity emerges out of a spirit of joy and trust that exults in the freedom of letting go. But at the same time Mennonites assume that attitudes will inevitably find expression in concrete actions. "From the one who has been entrusted with much," Jesus once said, "much more will be asked" (Luke 12:48).

Summary

In the Mennonite tradition Christian discipleship consciously accepts the responsibility of possessions. At the same time, it seeks to cultivate spiritual disciplines that will challenge the pressure of our culture to reduce human beings to the status of producers and consumers. We recognize that we are merely stewards, not owners, of God's bountiful blessings. Mennonites celebrate meaningful work. They seek to develop habits of extravagant generosity. They embrace simplicity. And they cultivate a recognition of our connectedness to the world around us, doing all of this as a joyful expression of gratitude to God.

8

Faith as Discipleship

Christian Practices in the Mennonite Tradition 2

Our Bodies: A Commitment to Fidelity and Trust

No less than the creative urge that drives human labor and productivity, the human body—with all of its natural appetites, desires, yearnings—is a gift from God. In the poetic language of Genesis, our mortal bodies, formed from the dust of the earth, have been given life by the very breath of God (2:7). We bear within ourselves the image and likeness of God and are part of the creation that God pronounced good! (1:26-31).

Part of our created nature is the freedom to make choices. This means that we are all unique beings, different from everyone else, and free to go our separate ways from each other and from God. Yet we also crave intimacy with other human beings and with God. So we live in a profound tension. As spiritual beings, we are united with every other human being by the image of God, recognizing in each person a common dignity and humanity. At the same time, we are unique individuals, possessing distinctive bodies, aware of our own individual mortality, and eager to preserve and protect our physical bodies by whatever means possible. We are hardwired, apparently, to defend ourselves; yet we are also aware—at least vaguely—that this human life counts for nothing compared to our spiritual identity as creatures bearing the image and likeness of God.

For much of Christian history, this dual awareness has played itself out as an ongoing battle between the human spirit and the body, with the dominant Christian attitude toward the body being one of deep suspicion. Many Christians have regarded the body as a kind of short-term prison for their spirit. Our bodies, after all, are the source of physical appetites and passions that cloud our spiritual vision and detract us from the Christian journey. As a result, the flesh must be subdued by a strong will and rigorous disciplines. This is the drama that Christians—especially Catholics—often reenact in the Lenten season prior to Easter. In Lent we consciously renounce the appetites of the body to demonstrate that they can be tamed and disciplined by a combination of human willpower and divine assistance. The extreme form of such an attitude is the ascetic tradition, where denying the pleasures of the body becomes a primary focus of Christian discipleship.

At the opposite extreme is the preoccupation that our contemporary culture has with the physical body, often to the point of hedonism (the pursuit of physical pleasure as an end in itself). In our culture hedonism finds expression as an obsession with consumption—especially food, alcohol, or various forms of entertainment—which often results in unhealthy bodies. Hedonism can also lead us to become fixated on the pursuit of an impossible quest for a perfect body, molded and sculpted by a rigorous regime of diets, health care products, and exercise, all in the hope that others will find us more attractive. Underneath it all is the throbbing subtext of sexual desire, in which thousands of advertisements, sitcoms, soap operas, movies, and Internet sites offer the alluring promise of intimacy and physical pleasure by gratifying our sexual yearnings. Given this intense cultural focus on our bodies, it should not surprise us that public debates over issues affecting our bodies—such as abortion, homosexual rights, fertility issues, and euthanasia—should be so heated.

Mennonites have not generally given the body much focused attention. If anything, they have been inclined toward the ascetic end of the spectrum, rather conservative in their personal ethics and suspicious of pleasure as a deviation from the narrow path of Christian discipleship. When Mennonites have addressed issues around the body, we have done so within the larger framework of Christian discipleship.

1. Stewardship of Our Body. Our bodies, writes the apostle Paul, are "a temple of the Holy Spirit" (1 Cor 6:19). We live in conversation with the Spirit, who inhabits our body. Yet even if we consider our deepest identity to be found in our spiritual rather than our physical being, we are still called to honor our bodies. This means that Christian disciples will give careful attention to the health of their bodies and the bodies of those around them. Mennonites, for example, are committed to feeding hungry people and offering clothing and shelter to those in need. Mennonites generally regard the use of cigarettes or illegal drugs as an abuse of the bodies God has entrusted to us. If they do consume alcohol, they believe it should be only in moderation and then with a sober awareness of its addictive potential.

Increasingly, Mennonite health-related groups are challenging members to be even more responsible for the stewardship of their bodies by encouraging healthy eating, more regular exercise, and better means of coping with stress. All of these practices communicate to God and to the world that we are only stewards of our bodies, charged with the responsibility of caring for them in thoughtful and respectful ways.

2. Celebrate Intimacy in the Context of Commitments. An essential part of being human is the deep desire to connect with other people—to reveal ourselves to others as we really are. Intimacy is a precious gift. It is precious precisely because the vulnerability and trust that make physical, emotional, and spiritual intimacy possible come at such a high risk. Exposing ourselves—our inner desires, foibles and faults, hopes and dreams, our physical bodies—can lead to pain if other people use what we reveal as a means of gaining power over us.

The intimacy of husband and wife or members of a congregational small group is premised on a prior commitment to God. Because Christian disciples have experienced intimacy with God—and know what it means to be loved in spite of our weaknesses and shortcomings—they are able to enter into similar relationships of trust and vulnerability with others. It is our shared commitment to Christ that makes possible shared commitments and intimacy with each other.

3. Sexual Intimacy Is Understood to Be Between Man and Woman in a Relationship of Marriage. The tendency in our culture to view human beings as mere bodies can easily have the effect of reducing intimacy to sexual relationships. From a Christian perspective, intimacy is clearly more than sexual intercourse. At the same time, however, God designed us as gendered beings—male and female—and gave us the gift of sexuality for both procreation and pleasure. Mennonites believe that sexuality is part of the goodness of God's creation. But its fullest expression—the intimacy of physical nakedness and intercourse—can be rightly appreciated only in the context of a lifelong commitment of marriage between a man and a woman. Of course there have been instances of Mennonite church people engaging in sexual intercourse outside of marriage. And the long-term consequences of such actions—pregnancy, shame, and a hesitancy to trust—deserve a response that goes beyond condemnation to compassion. At the same time, however, the church should denounce the popular illusion that people can engage in casual sexual relations without any negative outcomes. The response of the church should not be a puritanical imposition of rules but rather a clear affirmation of the gift of sexual intimacy within relationships of trust and commitment.

4. Homosexuality. Like many other denominations, the Mennonite church has recently engaged in a prolonged discussion about various issues related to homosexuality. Although a vocal minority have called on the church to bless gay marriages, most Mennonites are clearly supportive of the church's traditional teaching, which calls homosexuals to a life of celibacy and reserves the institution of marriage for a man and a woman. At the same time, however, the Mennonite church has denounced the homophobia of the broader culture and suggested that people of homosexual orientation may be included as full members of local congregations.

5. Families Are a Blessing; Singleness Is Affirmed. Traditionally, Mennonites have been known for their large extended families and for their habit—often irritating to new members—of initiating conversations by tracing networks of genealogical lineage. Mennonites clearly regard children as a blessing of God and honor families for their role in Christian nurture. Families are a crucial setting in which the spiritual formation of children occurs.

At the same time the church also acknowledges that some people, through choice or circumstance, remain single. This can also be a calling every bit as valued in the congregation as that of marriage. Indeed, the apostle Paul honored those who abstained from marriage, recognizing the singleness of purpose in Christian discipleship that these individuals enjoyed (1 Cor 7).

Perhaps the most distinctive Mennonite contribution to the topic of marriage and singleness is the conviction that the church —not our biological relatives—is our first family. There was a time when members of Mennonite congregations frequently referred to each other with the language of brother and sister. Although that custom is now slowly dying out, it has served as an important reminder—as did the practice of seating men and women on opposite sides of the church—that our identity as believers is more foundational than our identity as members of a particular family. Jesus was uncomfortably clear about this point: "Anyone who loves his father or mother more than me is not worthy of me" (Matt 10:37). It is not that families are a burden, but that part of living in anticipation of the new creation is a view of relationships that moves us beyond the comfortable boundaries of kinship ties. As our brothers and sisters in Christ, the congregation lays the same claims on my time, resources, love, and energy as does my biological family.

Power: A Commitment to Love, Nonviolence, and Service

At the heart of the Mennonite understanding of Christian discipleship and the new creation are Christ's teachings in the Gospels regarding love and service. In the Sermon on the Mount Jesus (Matt 5-7) calls his listeners to a pattern of morality that transcends mere justice or common sense or even the golden rule (7:12). Mennonite theological distinctives likely become most apparent in this commitment to demonstrating love in all human relations.

The Gospels report that throughout his ministry Jesus consistently challenges his followers to rethink a whole set of assumptions about status, power, security, and success that once seemed self-evident and obvious. It is not the wealthy or the powerful or the strong who are blessed by God, he teaches, but rather the poor in spirit, the meek, the pure in heart, those who are merciful (Matt 5). In this new way of life, the "first will be last, and the last first" (Mark 10:31). To enter this kingdom, we need to become like a child. If we want to be great in this kingdom, Jesus says, be a servant. If we want to save our life, lose it.

Perhaps no point is more foundational to this new orientation than Christ's admonition to love our enemies (Matt 5:44; Luke 6:27, 35; cf. Rom 12:17-21). It would seem much more logical, of course, to argue that we should defend our interests, punish those who threaten us, draw a line between good and evil, and give evildoers what they have coming to them. Yet, as Jesus makes clear in the Sermon on the Mount, there is no particular virtue in loving those who love you. It requires no special calling for us to love only our neighbors or those people who share our basic values. Indeed, there is nothing uniquely Christian about arguments defending violence so long as the cause is just. Just-war arguments remind us of principles such as fairness and justice, which are not bad things in and of themselves. But these principles do not necessarily point us to the gospel—to the stupendous, life-changing fact that God loves us, in spite of the fact that we don't deserve it. Christ teaches his disciples to love even those who persecute them, or mistreat them, or are their enemies. "Love your enemies and pray for those who persecute you, that you may be children of your Father in heaven" (Matt 5:44).

Mennonites are not suggesting by this interpretation that Jesus was powerless or that Jesus gave up his authority. Christian pacifism is not an invitation to a timid sort of passivity. But he explicitly challenged the human definition of power. The cross and resurrection, as Paul repeatedly declared in his letters, is a kind of power that "is made perfect in weakness" (2 Cor 12:9).

Most importantly, the cross was not the end of the story. Indeed, for Christians, the cross is actually only the beginning of the story. In the resurrection that followed, God made it clear that death and violence do not have the final word. Our fear that death is the worst thing that can happen to us turns out to be rooted in the assumptions of the fallen world. In Jesus's resurrection Christians proclaim that life and love are more powerful than violence and death.

1. The Gospel of Peace Is Rooted in Grace. At the heart of the Mennonite commitment to an ethic of love and nonviolence is a simple and yet profound affirmation shared widely throughout the Christian church. God loves us even though we do not merit or deserve God's compassion. "While we were still sinners," writes Paul in Romans, "Christ died for us." A verse later Paul returns to this amazing point: "When we were God's enemies, we were reconciled to him through the death of his Son" (Rom 5:8, 10). The point is clear: God loved us preemptively. God loved us even while we were still rebelling against God, while we were still acting as if God mattered nothing to us. Thus, Mennonites are committed to loving our enemies not because it is heroic or will somehow bring God's favor. Rather, we are committed to live out the gospel of peace because this is exactly how God has treated us. Christians testify to the power of God's love in our lives to the extent that God's love for us becomes transparent in the way we treat others.

For the Christian committed to the path of discipleship with Jesus, this amazing realization becomes the basis for Christian ethics and mission. We give witness to God's grace only to the extent that we allow God's forgiving love to flow through us to embrace everyone we encounter, including—and one might add, *especially* including—those who are not worthy of that love, those we consider to be our enemies.

Too often the principle of nonviolence has been expressed in negative terms such as a refusal to go to war, a rejection of violence, or opposition to injustice. In a world deeply shaped by the logic of coercion, it is inevitable that Christians will often find themselves in opposition. But at the heart of the Mennonite witness to peace is a deep, warm, and joyful affirmation. I am called to love my enemies because that's exactly what God did to me. I cannot sing "Amazing Grace" with integrity until I am ready to extend that same grace— a grace that is greater than even the sins of my enemies—to those who have done nothing to deserve it.

2. The Gospel of Peace Is Neither Spiritual nor Political. Frequently, as the ideas of Christian peacemaking find their way into practice, Christians are tempted to translate the gospel of peace into terms that seem less radical or counter-cultural. Some Christians, for example, talk about peace primarily in personal or spiritual terms. When Jesus preached on peace, they suggest, he was referring to the state of spiritual harmony that Christians enjoy when they are at peace with God. This is a peace of the heart—an inner peace separate from the daily grind of human relationships. In fact, some would say, it is precisely this inner peace that allows the Christian to participate in the external horrors and violence of war.

Such a distinction between feelings of the heart and the deeds of the hands, however, is contrary to the teachings of Jesus and the New Testament. Jesus described as "foolish" anyone "who hears these words of mine and does not put them into practice" (Matt 7:26).

On the other hand, there are also Christians who understand the gospel of peace primarily as a motivational language to promote the political strategies of pacifism, often in association with the platform of a specific political party. Here the temptation is to use Jesus as an advocate for a particular political cause, often muting the language of conversion and resurrection because they sound embarrassingly Christian in public settings.

Mennonites have generally rejected both of these tendencies. The gospel of peace is more than just a warm inner spiritual feeling. But at the same time it is also more than a strategy of international diplomacy to enlist in the cause of a particular political goal.

3. *The Gospel of Peace Is Both Spiritual and Political.* Given what I have just explained above, this statement will almost certainly sound paradoxical, if not outright contradictory. Yet it is crucial to understand the distinction. The Mennonite understanding of peacemaking is strongly spiritual in the sense that it is grounded in God's action through Christ in demonstrating his love for the world. Mennonite peacemaking is grounded in an affirmation of the power of the resurrection over the forces of violence and death. When Mennonites advocate on behalf of reconciliation and peacemaking, we do so not because we think this is the most politically expedient way of getting to a particular outcome. In fact, there are no guarantees that responding nonviolently in the face of an aggressive person or nation will stop the aggressors in their tracks, at least not in the short term. But Mennonites affirm a spiritual reality at work that is deeper and truer and more real than the aggression presenting itself at the moment. And we participate with Christ in the path of discipleship when we respond to hatred with love, or when we resist evildoers without taking on the tactics of the evildoers we are resisting. This is a deeply spiritual claim. The martyrs died, not chanting political slogans, but singing hymns, preaching the good news of the gospel, and confessing their faith.

At the same time, however, the gospel of peace is profoundly political in the sense that it *engages* the world by standing in the way of evildoing and violence. The gospel of peace, as Mennonites have understood it, is not a passive retreat from the forces of evil. After all, Jesus confronted the principalities and powers by proclaiming the "kingdom" of God, and his followers acknowledged him as "Lord"—both words that have strong political overtones. Moreover, Roman and Jewish authorities regarded Jesus as such a political threat that they cooperated in having him put to death. Their fears were politically motivated, and Jesus did not strenuously resist this characterization of him as a king. But the nature of his "political" activity completely confounded those around him, including the disciples. When he made his triumphal entry into the capital city, he came riding on a donkey. When Peter tried to resist Jesus's arrest in the garden of Gethsemane, Jesus ordered him to put away his sword, and he immediately healed the wound Peter had inflicted. When faced with the prospects of calling down an army of warrior angels to avenge the false charges and his sham trial and wrongful conviction, Jesus choose instead to ask God to "forgive them, for they do not know what they are doing" (Luke 23:34). This was the nature of Jesus's political actions.

Mennonites have traditionally been respectful of civil authorities and have sought ways of peaceful coexistence. But when bearing witness to their understanding of the gospel of peace has brought them into conflict with authorities, they have presented themselves not as partisans in the standard political debates of the democratic process, but as people giving a testimony to a better way.

4. Jesus Is Lord: Qualified Allegiance to the State. Mennonites are deeply appreciative of their country. We celebrate the opportunities it affords for self-expression, and we delight in the natural beauty of this wonderful land. But Mennonites are likely to cringe when they hear other Christians echo the slogan "God bless America." They do so not because God is indifferent to America, but because such sloganeering so easily becomes a way for us to reshape God into *our* image and assume that God somehow cares about us more than about people elsewhere in the world. The gospel of peace reminds us that Jesus is Lord of the whole world, and that our allegiance to the body of Christ comes before our allegiance to the nation. It calls us to take seriously the claim in the familiar hymn by John Oxenham that "in Christ there is no East or West, in him no South or North, but one great fellowship of love throughout the whole wide earth."

5. Consistently Pro-Life. Mennonites have not always been in agreement about how they should address the government on this issue, but the overwhelming majority reject abortion as a personal option. Sidestepping the debate over precisely when a fetus becomes a human being, most Mennonites see abortion as inconsistent with their commitment to the sanctity of life as God's good gift. Mennonite opposition to capital punishment on the other hand, has been somewhat more ambiguous. Many have spoken out strongly against the death penalty. Yet some have argued that the state—as part of a fallen world that routinely trains citizens to kill in times of war—will inevitably use lethal violence in fulfilling its mandate of Romans 13 to protect the good and punish evil. In any event, the Christian witness always moves in the direction of God's extravagant love and toward the sanctity of human life.

6. Service as an Expression of the Gospel of Peace. Perhaps the most consistent way that Mennonites have tried to live out the principles of the gospel of peace is by cultivating the practice of service. Mennonite understandings of service include a wide variety of programs, many of them intended for young people as they pursue clarity in their life's vocation. Options for service cover an enormous range of possibilities in domestic and international settings, urban areas and small towns, by engaging in social service, construction, urban renewal, youth work, and medical missions, to name only a few options. Some Mennonite service programs are self-consciously oriented to Christian missions. Others extend service in the name of Christ but are not as aggressive in promoting the Christian faith. In both instances, however, Christian service is marked by a readiness to move into areas of human need and pain and to become the light of Christ by extending a hand to those in need. Christian service assumes a posture of humility; it seeks to meet people where they live. And almost inevitably, the transformation is mutual. In serving others, we encounter Christ and we find that we have been served.

Summary: Walking in the Resurrection

In the hit movie, *The Passion of the Christ*, director Mel Gibson chose to depict the suffering of Jesus in the hours leading up to his death in vivid, graphic detail. No one seeing the movie could leave without a deep awareness of the sheer pain and physical brutality that Jesus endured in his slow, agonizing death on the cross. From this perspective, a Mennonite would likely affirm the movie for its sobering reminder that the path of discipleship is not easy. Though he did not pose as a militant revolutionary, Jesus's life and teachings clearly struck a nerve in both the Roman and Jewish establishment. Those who follow after him should not be surprised if they encounter resistance from the surrounding culture. Baptism, as Paul writes, is a "baptism into death" (Rom 6:4)

Less clear in the movie, however, was the place of the resurrection in the story of Christ's passion. For Mennonites, the real focus of the Easter story is not primarily Christ's gruesome and painful death. Rather, Easter is a celebration of the fact that violence and death do not have the last word. Christians, after all, are post-resurrection followers of Christ. We have been redeemed by Christ, transformed by the power of God's love, and are called to walk in the power of the resurrection. Precisely because of the resurrection, we bear witness to a different reality than the logic of force that led to Christ's death.

By holding up the light of the gospel of peace, Christians testify to the world that the darkness of violence will not prevail. The gospel of peace proclaims that the resurrection will triumph over the cross. It proclaims that allegiance to the body of Christ comes before our allegiance to the nation-state. And it proclaims that history is ultimately shaped "not by [human] might nor by power," but by the Spirit of the living God (Zech 4:6).

9

Faith as Discipleship

A Critique... and Ongoing Questions

Mennonites are certainly not unique in their emphasis on discipleship as an integral part of Christian faith. All Christian groups, Catholic and Protestant alike, teach that faith is linked to ethical behavior. Yet Mennonites believe that the Christian life points to a *qualitatively* different way of being in the world, a way of life that will inevitably distinguish believers from society in general. This assertion was offensive to many people in the sixteenth century, and it remains troubling to many Christians today.

The Problem of Perfectionism

The Mennonite emphasis on practical Christian discipleship is a good thing, some critics say, and perhaps even admirable. But behind all this attention on putting one's faith into action is the dangerous assumption that Christians can actually live up to the standard of Christ. Yet, as we know from experience, even the most sincere Christian is still far from the perfection that Christ seems to demand in the Sermon on the Mount. For all of their high-minded ideals, the truth of the matter is that Mennonites do not follow the teachings of Jesus literally. None of them literally adheres to Jesus's command to be "perfect, … even as your heavenly Father is perfect" (Matt 5:48)!

Already in the sixteenth century Luther recognized an inherent dilemma in the Christian life when he insisted that a Christian is "simultaneously righteous and a sinner" (*simul justus et peccator*). In other words, just because we have been baptized and consciously desire to follow Jesus does not mean that we have ceased to sin. In fact, Christians who try to live absolutely pure lives are either deluding themselves or will quickly be driven by their shortcomings back again into the arms of grace. The Anabaptist emphasis on good works, Luther and other reformers claimed, was simply creating a new form of monasticism that led to the arrogance and delusion of perfectionism.

Most Mennonites today would readily accept that their lives are far from the perfection of Christ. And they would probably agree with Luther that the phrase "simultaneously righteous and a sinner" is an accurate description of how we often live. But, they respond, acknowledging these points is hardly an adequate basis for developing an ethic for how Christians should live. Luther's *simul justus et peccator* might describe how we actually *are* (we know, for example, that humans have a tendency to be greedy). But this observation dare not become a justification for sin (implying that greed is an appropriate way of behaving). Christian ethics should point us in the direction of how we *ought* to live, not provide a justification for our tendency to sin. Or, to put it another way, arguing from the outset that it is impossible for us to reach a standard seems to justify the status quo or become a rationale for giving up pursuit of the goal.

Mennonites would do well to be more forthright in acknowledging their imperfections and their absolute dependence on God's mercy and grace. But by the same token, the temptation of "cheap grace"—a view of grace that justifies the sin rather than the sinner—is extremely powerful in American Christianity. Mennonites believe that Christians should vigilantly avoid this temptation.

The Gospel of Peace Makes Mennonites Parasites on the Civil Order

As a child, I was the only Mennonite in my small-town elementary school class. When my friends invited me into their homes to play, I often noticed pictures of young men—fathers, brothers, uncles—in military uniform, proudly displayed on their living room walls. One day the father of one of my friends, a pastor in a local church, made a special point of calling my attention to a picture of his brother. "You pacifists," he said with an anger I had never earlier heard in him, "you pacifists don't know what it means to sacrifice on behalf of our country! Yet here you are enjoying the same freedoms as everyone else. You're nothing but a bunch of parasites."

His words stunned me. I had always been proud of the fact that my grandfather had successfully resisted pressure to put on a military uniform when he had been forced to report for duty to a World War I training camp in camp in Chillicothe, Ohio. I had always thought of those martyrs in the Anabaptist tradition as courageous heroes, not as parasites. Yet through the years, some observers have repeatedly raised the charge that Mennonite conscientious objectors to war selfishly benefit by the political order and stability guaranteed by the U.S. military or the police force. It is a charge worth taking seriously.

By and large, Mennonites regard the state—and its role of preserving order in a violent world—with deep respect. In Romans 13, the apostle Paul describes the state as "God's servant, an agent of wrath to bring punishment on the wrongdoer" (Rom 13:4). For many Christians, this passage is the foundation for defending government as a Christian institution. Mennonites take the point seriously, but they caution other Christians to read carefully what is stated in this passage and what is not.

The context for Paul's reflections on the state actually begins in chapter 12 with a series of instructions to Christians for holy living. Included in the admonitions are teachings that explicitly invoke the gospel of peace: "Bless those who persecute you; bless and do not curse" (12:14). "Do not repay anyone evil for evil" (12:17). "Do not take revenge, my friends; . . . on the contrary: 'If your enemy is hungry, feed him; if he is thirsty, give him something to drink'" (12:19-20). "Do not be overcome by evil, but overcome evil with good" (12:21). What follows in chapter 13, then, are instructions for how Christians should relate to government authorities. But there is no assumption that these authorities are themselves Christians (in Paul's day, the Roman authorities were definitely *not* Christians). So Paul is not assuming that those in power are followers of Christ. Still, he wants to make clear to believers that they do have some obligations to these officials. God has given the state authority to bring order into human society. Order in a fallen world—even an order that depends ultimately on the sword—is better than chaos and anarchy. So Christians should respect that order and give the state its due.

Note, however, that this is not the same thing as saying that Christians should either participate in government or do whatever the government tells them to do. In the end, Christians "must obey God rather than men!" (Acts 5:29).

From a Mennonite perspective, all of this means that we recognize with gratitude the role of the state in preserving order. But we do not assume that the state is in itself "Christian," nor that Christians are the ones who should be creating this kind of order in a fallen world. On the contrary, Christians are called to live by an altogether different standard—a standard described in Romans 12. For Christians, "Jesus is Lord," not Caesar (10:9). And that means that they will live in accordance with the principles of the new creation, principles based on a love that extends even to the enemy.

Mennonites Are Naive About the Reality of Evil in the World

There is a long-standing and unfortunate tradition within the broader Christian church of assuming that Christians who believe in nonviolence are promoting a so-called "social gospel" that is naively optimistic about human nature and the power of human reason to resolve all social problems. Christian pacifists, the argument goes, think that if people are only "nice" to tyrants and dictators, the evildoers of the world will suddenly repent of their sins, lay down their weapons, and start acting with compassion and generosity.

While it is true that some Mennonites may do or say things that give this impression, such a view does not reflect the mainstream of Mennonite theology. Most Mennonites are "realists" in their recognition of the nature of evil in the world. That is precisely why Mennonites give so much attention to the nature of a "new life in Christ" and why the stakes involved in becoming a Christian are so high.

But Mennonites also believe that the resurrection—not the cross—has the last word in human history. In Christ, God has demonstrated his power over the forces of evil and death. In a cosmic sense, the victory over the "principalities and powers" has already been won. Christians are called to live—albeit imperfectly—in the light of this truth.

The optimism of Mennonites regarding the gospel of peace is therefore not grounded in a confidence in the human ability to create a peaceful world order. Instead, it is grounded in the faith that God became known most fully to the world in a posture of vulnerability and love. We believe that the way of the cross will eventually lead to life.

Ongoing Questions Among Mennonites Today

1. Is the Primary Focus of Christian Discipleship on Personal Morality or Social Justice? Mennonites today are not always of one mind as to whether the primary focus of Christian discipleship should be on matters of personal morality or larger questions of social justice. Traditionally, Mennonites have taken a fairly strict view on personal virtues, upholding behaviors like honesty, trustworthiness, sexual fidelity, and charity to those in need. In many local settings, the Mennonite reputation for high standards of personal morality and ethics has been a powerful form of witness.

More recently, however, Mennonites have also begun to develop a growing awareness of the structural forms that sin can take, especially as it is expressed in various kinds of social injustice. For example, the Jim Crow laws in the South that systematically discriminated against African-Americans were changed only because people of faith challenged the sinful nature of an entire set of laws. When poor people die prematurely because they do not have access to health care, the flaws of that system will not be fixed by acts of local charity alone. And so a growing number of Mennonites have begun to bear witness to their convictions in more public ways, including political activism. Still, even though most Mennonites would acknowledge the importance of both personal and social ethics, congregations are sometimes divided as to which of these should be the primary focus of discipleship.

The dangers of becoming locked into either side of this equation are clear. Those whose attention is focused primarily on the structural level can easily become caught up in the secular perspectives and language of the social sciences in their quest for social reforms. As a result, they may ignore the spiritual component of their work, forgetting that the battle is, in some important ways, against "the principalities and powers" of evil. In locating the heart of the world's problems in an abstract system, external to the individual, social reformers can also overlook or minimize the importance of personal choices and the cultivation of individual practices and disciplines.

By the same token, a preoccupation on personal morality can easily become a safe retreat from the deeper and more complex problems of the world. It is easier, for example, to discipline oneself not to drink alcohol than to become engaged in the messy details of running an alcohol-recovery program, or to challenge the advertising industry for directing alcohol commercials to urban young people. We are powerfully tempted to say, "If it is not affecting me personally, then it doesn't really matter." Though the specific topics vary widely, this larger tension about the nature of our public witness is a point of continuing conversation and debate within Mennonite circles.

2. Is the Commitment to Nonviolence Absolute? Most Mennonites recognize the many and varied forms that violence can take in our world. And though their opposition to lethal violence is firm and their commitment to peacemaking is clear, they often find themselves struggling to sort out appropriate responses to other forms of violence. In the end, many Mennonites would stop short of saying that every imaginable form of applied force is absolutely wrong. For example, no Mennonite would argue that a Christian should look on piously while a deranged person attacks a child. Clearly, some form of intervention or restraint would be appropriate. Many Mennonite parents—though not all—have spanked their children on occasion. And few would respond to the classic question "What would you do if someone broke into your home and was threatening to injure your family?" by saying that the only acceptable option is to drop to our knees and pray.

In these circumstances, we cannot always see a clear line separating legitimate forms of intervention on behalf of innocent people from unchristian acts of coercive violence. What is clear for Mennonites, however, is the line separating us from using *lethal* violence. A Mennonite cannot in good conscience willfully destroy the life of another human being who is made in the image of God, no matter how evil their actions may appear to be. A commitment to the gospel of peace should not be understood as a withdrawal from all forms of social or ethical responsibility. But the overwhelming presumption for Mennonites remains on the side of peace and love. And the most crucial line is drawn at the point of killing someone else.

3. What Are Appropriate Expressions of Patriotism? Variations on this question arise in countless settings. What do Mennonites say to friends and neighbors who speak proudly about their children in the armed forces or want to know our opinion about a current war? How do Mennonites respond during the pledge of allegiance at the local PTO or Rotary Club meetings? What about the national anthem played before the local high school basketball games? What about a neighborhood initiative to fly the flag from every porch on Memorial Day? On these and many similar questions, Mennonites are likely to respond in a wide variety of ways. A few might be as enthusiastically patriotic as their next-door neighbor, unabashedly proud to be "a red-blooded American." Other Mennonites look for ways of showing respect for their country while still symbolically reminding themselves (and others) that their primary allegiance belongs to God and the international church. Thus, they might stand respectfully during the pledge or the national anthem, but not put their hand over their heart or participate orally. Or they might express personal interest in the safety of a relative in the armed forces while also stating deep reservations about the war in general. Some Mennonites, on the other hand, feel called to give a clearer public and prophetic witness against the idolatry of nation-alism wherever they can, even if those around them might regard their actions as offensive.

The official position of the Mennonite church is clearly opposed to members participating in the armed services. But on the complex questions of patriotism and the symbols of national allegiance, many of which are closely related to the language of military defense and sacrifice, Mennonites are more equivocal.

4. What Does It Actually Mean to "Live Simply"? Not long ago, a caller to the well-known NPR radio talk show *Click and Clack* identified herself as a Mennonite with a moral and spiritual problem related to her car. The car she was currently driving, she explained, was a beat-up "clunker" that, unfortunately, was still in fine running condition. Such a car was consistent with a Mennonite ethic of simplicity, frugality, and good stewardship. Her spiritual problem, she confided, came in the fact that she had fallen in love with the thought of owning a brand new Toyota Prius—a car that she really liked. The Prius promised great gas mileage and was ecologically friendly. But it was also quite expensive, and her old car showed no signs of imminent problems. Was she justified in buying a new car?

In the end, the Tappet brothers, amid lots of good-natured laughter, advised her to resolve the problem by changing denominations. The exchange was all in good humor, but it focused a difficult question. What are the appropriate standards for a simple lifestyle? Perhaps more vexing, what is the appropriate point of comparison in making decisions about consumer spending? Even if we conscientiously resist the impulse of recreational shopping and the consumerist mentality of our culture, we are still likely to be enormously wealthier than the majority of those living in the world's Southern Hemisphere. Buying food at the local farmers' market may be healthier, but it's also likely to be more expensive. How do we weigh the stewardship of time gained in the convenience of buying from Wal-Mart against the far less tangible benefits of driving further and paying more to support a locally owned hardware? For most of the world's population, health insurance is an unthinkable luxury. For many of America's poor, it is ardent hope. For professionals, it is simply an assumed benefit of the job. Should white-collar Mennonites give up their health insurance as an act of solidarity with the poor?

In short, simple living is not simple at all. And on these issues, Mennonites are clearly not of one mind. Some are quite happy to enjoy the pleasures of conspicuous consumption, grateful to God for the bounty of a prosperous life. Others seek symbolic gestures of resistance: buying fair-trade coffee, for example, will not transform the nature of the global economy, but it reminds us that we are indeed connected to those distant producers and it might help boost the income of a few farm laborers. Still other Mennonites have chosen lives of international service or voluntary poverty as a way of identifying with the poor. In each instance, however, the meaning of "simple living" clearly remains a matter of ongoing discussion and some disagreement among contemporary Mennonites.

5. What About Divorce and Remarriage? As we have seen, Mennonites place a high value on marriage and the commitment of fidelity at the heart of the marriage vow. As witnessed by the congregation and the gathering of family and friends, we take seriously the sacred nature of this promise: "What God has joined together, let no one put asunder" (cf. Mark 10:9).

Yet the reality is that that some marriages fail, even in Mennonite congregations. Fifty years ago divorce was virtually unheard of within the Mennonite church. Today, a growing number of Mennonites, though far less than national average, opt for divorce.

The Mennonite church is not entirely of one mind about the appropriate response to failed marriages. Some congregations intervene strenuously on behalf of the marriage and regard divorce as a clear moral failure, for both husband and wife as well as for the congregation. Others are more apt to respond with sadness but not to look on divorce as a matter for church intervention or discipline. Many congregations, though not all, accept the remarriage of divorced people, albeit with a heavy heart in light of the scriptural injunctions.

Summary

In these, as in many other issues, Mennonites frequently find themselves in intense conversation, debate, and even outright disagreement. Such tensions have been both a weakness and a strength within the Mennonite tradition. At its worst, this impulse in the Mennonite tradition to take ethics seriously can easily lead to legalism, a contentious spirit, and a readiness to part ways in the name of truth and purity. Over the centuries, groups in the Anabaptist-Mennonite tradition have frequently splintered and divided, not so much over points of theological doctrine as over issues related to ethical practice. Too often, Paul's admonition to the church at Ephesus to be a church "without spot or wrinkle" (cf. Eph 5:27, KJV) has justified divisions within the body of Christ that have estranged family and neighbors.

At its best, however, the Mennonite understanding of faith as inextricably linked to a life of discipleship has prevented them from falling into the trap of "cheap grace" that seems so prevalent in much of American Christianity. For Mennonites, faith is an empty abstraction until it is embodied in daily life. Ethical practices are not, as some Christian traditions seem to suggest, a kind of "accessory" that one adds sometime following the more foundational experience of salvation. To put it in a slightly different way, salvation in the Mennonite tradition is not something that you "have," like an absentee landlord who keeps the deed to a property stored in a safe. Rather, salvation is something that must be lived. You own the property only if you actually live there, cultivate the land, and make it a central part of your daily life. Similarly, believers cannot truly claim to have experienced God's love and forgiveness if they are not ready to extend that love and forgiveness in concrete ways to those around them.

This may open Mennonites to the charge of "works righteousness"—thinking that one's good deeds will bring favor with God. Yet most would simply respond by saying that God's grace not only forgives; it also empowers. In the words of one Anabaptist writer, "No one can truly know Christ except one who follows him in life."

For Mennonites, the life of discipleship is not for rugged individualists. Discipleship always unfolds within the context of a larger group of committed believers who are also struggling to discern God's will and conform their lives to the teachings of Jesus. It is appropriate, then, that we now turn to the church, a central theme of Christian faith and practice in the Mennonite tradition.

10

The Visible Church

Commitment and Worship

In the spring of 1974, a devastating tornado ripped through the town of Xenia in southern Ohio, killing 33 people and destroying more than 1,600 buildings. I was a 14-year-old boy at the time, an awkward adolescent and unsure about a lot of things. I found the news of the tornado to be deeply troubling. In this random act of nature, why did the tornado's path suddenly veer into the town? Did God plan such events or merely allow them to happen? I could understand that sinful people were forced to live with the consequences of bad choices. But the destruction of a town of 25,000 people seemed like an arbitrary act of evil that God should have prevented.

As I followed the story in the newspaper, my small congregation sixty miles away began to organize a crew to assist the larger efforts of Mennonite Disaster Service in the cleanup. As the crew formed, one of the older men in the congregation called my father one evening to ask whether I might be able to join them for the eight-day effort. I was shocked—first that the men of the church would have thought to include me in the crew, but even more that my parents would allow me to join them even though it meant missing a full week of school.

In retrospect, the week of work in Xenia was a formative moment in my life. Clearing away debris and talking with survivors of the tragedy gave me a tangible way to work through some of my questions about the nature of evil. The experience broadened my horizons and made me aware that people in other denominations were also eagerly responding to the tragedy. Mennonites were not the only ones who were ready to put their faith into action. But most of all, working alongside other men in my congregation sealed for me a deep conviction that I was an important part of my local church. I was representing all the members of our little congregation, and my contribution mattered. At the same time, the work crew from church became an extension of my family. We worked, prayed, ate, and joked together, forging bonds of friendship that lingered long after our return.

That awareness of the centrality of the local congregation to my understanding of the Christian faith would recur often in the coming years—especially in the aftermath of a devastating house fire and the death of my youngest brother from cancer. But April of 1974 stands out most clearly as the moment of my realization that the church mattered to me.

According to a recent poll, more than 50 percent of Americans attend church on a regular basis. Though the figure has declined somewhat over the past decade, it continues to stand in sharp contrast to Europe, where church attendance is less than 15 percent in most countries (a mere 5 percent in the Scandinavian countries!). Visible evidence of the importance of the church to American religious life is present almost anywhere one looks. From the small urban storefront congregation in the heart of the city to the sprawling megachurch complex just off the interstate bypass, from the isolated country chapel at the corner of a Midwestern cornfield to the majestic reach of the cathedral's spire—church buildings are an inescapable feature of the American landscape. The phone book of almost every North American hamlet and town bears further witness to the enormous variety of choices enjoyed by churchgoers today. Clearly, most people in North America continue to assume that their personal convictions regarding Christian faith are linked in some important way to the rituals of gathering and worship with a larger group of believers.

This abundant variety of religious choices—the range of beliefs, worship styles, architectural design, and program options—would have been utterly unthinkable to a European peasant in the late fifteenth century. At the time of the Reformation, the basic outlines of the church had been firmly established for nearly a millennium. The Catholic church, headed by the pope in Rome, was universal in its spiritual presence and authority, and it was unified—at least theoretically—in its theology. Throughout all of Europe the liturgy of the mass was spoken in the same language (Latin) following the same basic pattern. The church understood itself to be the living body of Christ, and the body of Christ could not be divided.

All of this changed dramatically with the advent of the Reformation. In the first half of the sixteenth century, Martin Luther, Ulrich Zwingli, John Calvin, and dozens of other reformers challenged the universal authority of the Catholic church by introducing new, alternative ways of believing and worshipping. Luther and his followers, for example, translated the ceremony of the mass into German so that everyone could understand it. They rejected the traditional Catholic focus on relics and images of saints, along with other "external" aspects of faith that they thought detracted believers from the inward reality of God's grace. They emphasized the authority of Scripture over the pope's authority. And they elevated the sermon as a focal point of Christian worship. Calvin and those in the Reformed tradition tended to simplify worship practices and worship spaces even more, eliminating all visual distractions and restricting singing to the Psalms set to music.

Despite all these changes, some aspects of the medieval church remained unaltered by the Reformation. Both the Lutheran and Reformed churches, for example, continued the medieval practice of infant baptism. Salvation, they believed, was a gift conferred on the infant at birth, not the result of a conscious decision made by the believer to follow Jesus. By the same token, both the Lutheran and the Reformed tradition continued to assume that the church and the state were intimately bound to each other. Indeed, now that the church could no longer realistically claim to be "universal" in its authority, the role of the state loomed even larger for Protestant denominations than it had during the Catholic Middle Ages. When Catholic, Lutheran, and Reformed believers found themselves locked in bitter religious warfare against each other, all parties eventually agreed to a solution of granting each territorial prince the right to determine the religion of his subjects. In practical terms, this principle of "whose region, his religion" (*cuius regio, eius religio*) meant that the prince—not the bishop—held ultimate authority over the church of his land since he possessed the right to impose unity in matters of religion, using force if necessary.

So underneath the flurry of reforms in the sixteenth century, other basic assumptions regarding the nature of the church continued to remain unchanged. In a real way, the medieval fusion of religion, politics, and culture—what historians sometimes refer to as Christendom—continued well beyond the time of the Reformation.

The Anabaptist Alternative

In their embrace of the principle of Scripture alone and in their rejection of the Catholic hierarchy, the Anabaptists of the sixteenth century shared much with the Protestant reformers. But in several other key areas—including their understanding of the church—the Anabaptists insisted that the reformers had not gone far enough. The Anabaptists agreed with Luther that salvation was indeed a gift but counted it as a gift that needed to be actively accepted. And once accepted, God's grace needed to bear fruit in the life of the new Christian. Since babies could neither consciously choose to accept God's grace nor live a regenerated life, the Anabaptists rejected the practice of infant baptism.

These convictions all had profound consequences for how the

Anabaptists understood the church. For if the church was comprised of members who had joined it voluntarily, then it could no longer be regarded as an institution whose identity was defined by the state and the dominant culture. For the Anabaptists, the voluntary nature of faith necessarily implied the separation of church and state. They understood that the Christian life would be in tension with the surrounding culture.

Mennonite Understandings of the Two Kingdoms

Mennonites have sometimes described this new understanding of the church using the language of two kingdoms. The concept of the two kingdoms begins with the recognition that all of creation is engaged in a cosmic battle, a spiritual warfare between good and evil. Since the story of the fall in Genesis 3, salvation history—the unfolding record of God's actions in the Old Testament and New Testament—is a dramatic account of the persistent struggle between faithfulness to God's intentions for the world and the stubborn reality of human selfishness, greed, and violence. This struggle gives meaning to the language of sin, salvation, and redemption. It reminds us that something of utmost importance is at stake. Even though Christians know that the ultimate outcome of this battle has already been decided—the resurrection confirms Christ's victory over the powers of death—we nonetheless find ourselves faced with a genuine choice.

The significance of this choice is underscored throughout the New Testament. Jesus tells his disciples that a follower of his cannot serve two masters: "Either he will hate the one and love other, or he will be devoted to the one and despise the other" (Matt 6:24). Paul echoes this theme when he urges the church in Rome, "Do not conform any longer to the pattern of this world," but rather "be transformed by the renewing of your mind" (Rom 12:2). In a similar vein, James says, "Don't you know that friendship with the world is hatred toward God? Anyone who *chooses* to be a friend of the world becomes an enemy of God" (4:4). The persecution faced by the early Christians only further dramatized the urgent nature of the choice. No one was "born" into the early church; those who choose to become members were literally putting their lives on the line.

This, then, is the context for the Mennonite understanding of the church. The church is made up of those people who have consciously committed themselves—imperfectly, to be sure—to orient their lives in the direction of the new creation, following the lead of Jesus's teachings and the model of the early church.

As a consequence, the church inevitably has a social, economic, and political form that is visibly distinct from the surrounding society. If the focus of a Catholic service is the celebration of the mass and the focus of a Protestant service is the sermon ("the Word rightly preached"), Mennonites are more likely to describe their church in less dramatic aspects of congregational life that give the church its concrete shape. While rituals and sermons are important aspects of worship, the presence of the Spirit is also revealed, claim Mennonites, in the practices of congregational life that give the body of Christ a tangible shape and form.

Practices that shape the life of a Mennonite church can be as simple as the greetings members extend to each other upon entering the church. They find expression in the way the offering is collected, in the sharing of congregational concerns, in the tradition of opening homes to newcomers for a meal or the occasional invitation to kneel for prayer. Practices can also be more formalized, such as a ritual of anointing, or a service of communion and foot washing, where we literally reenact a practice that Jesus passed along to his disciples. Practices always have a concrete expression, but they are intended to point us beyond ourselves to the group and, ultimately, to God.

To summarize: a Mennonite congregation is made up of people who have publicly offered their primary allegiance to Christ—not to a state, a social class, a set of political principles, or even to a fixed list of nonnegotiable doctrinal principles. Though never perfect, the church is made visible through a series of concrete practices that reflect the teachings of Jesus, testify to the presence of the Spirit, and point toward the coming kingdom of God, when God's intentions for all humanity will be fully realized.

Anabaptist-Mennonite Worship

Perhaps the most basic practice of a Mennonite church is that of worship. We sometimes think of worship in a fairly narrow sense of regular gatherings structured around events like singing, Scripture, preaching, communion, and prayer. But Mennonites believe that since all of life is under the reign of God, regardless of the setting or the focus of their activities, they are engaged in an act of worship, whenever and wherever God's people gather.

Compared with many other Christian traditions, worship in Mennonite settings generally tends toward an informal (low church) style. Many congregations have long-established customs regarding the proper components, order, and tone of a worship service, so that the service can appear to unfold in a ritual-like fashion. Yet most Mennonite churches do not follow a denominationally prescribed liturgy or elevate certain sacred rituals to a level of prominence. Thus, visitors from Catholic or Episcopal traditions are likely to find Mennonite worship to seem somewhat casual or even haphazard in its structure.

This bias toward a more simple style of worship, in which laypersons often play a prominent role, reflects the anticlerical roots of the early Anabaptist movement. In keeping with the sixteenth-century practice of worshipping in homes, barns, caves, or forest clearings, Mennonites have traditionally favored plain and simple settings for worship. Pastors do not wear robes or vestments that set them apart from the laity, and pulpits tend to be only slightly elevated above the seating level of the congregation. Even after tolerant princes in Europe permitted them to have buildings of their own, Mennonites tended to construct highly functional and often austere meetinghouses instead of buildings that aspired to architectural grandeur. This practice has changed dramatically in recent decades, with a growing number of Mennonite congregations ready to hire architects and to invest significant amounts of money into their church buildings. Nevertheless, Mennonites still tend to prefer structures with lots of multipurpose spaces and they are likely to commit more resources to foyers and fellowship halls than to altars, choir lofts, and stained-glass windows. Some contemporary Mennonite congregations have opted to orient the worship space in the form of a circle. The purpose is to heighten a sense of community, with the focal point on the people gathered for worship rather than on a pulpit or altar.

The structure of a typical Mennonite worship service inevitably varies, especially with the recent growth of the Mennonite church among immigrant populations in large urban areas. On any given Sunday in Philadelphia, for example, one could attend a Mennonite service in nearly twenty different languages. Each has a worship style that inevitably reflects something of the cultural tradition of the participants. The description of worship that follows below is based largely on a traditional English-speaking Mennonite service, the group that is numerically dominant in North America. But it by no means is the only model of authentic Mennonite worship.

Many Mennonite congregations have long cultivated a deep appreciation for singing, especially four-part chorales and hymns. There was a time, especially among Mennonites in the Swiss-South German tradition, when all instruments were banned as worldly distractions from worship. Those concerns are now distant memories. Most congregations have a piano or organ and frequently use other instruments to accompany congregational singing. Singing, of course, is common to the whole Christian tradition. Among Mennonites, however, the practice of four-part a cappella singing has become a central part of congregational identity, holding theological significance as a communal event that joins individual voices into a harmonious unity.

A layperson will often read the Scripture before the sermon. Although a few congregations have begun to follow the common lectionary in the selection of scriptural passages, more typically the preacher or the worship committee chooses a Scripture that reflects the theme of the sermon. Preaching is usually the task of the minister, though it is also not uncommon to have another member give the sermon. As in other denominations, Mennonite preaching ranges widely in style and content. A sermon may be exegetical or topical and delivered extemporaneously or read from a prepared text. Mennonite preaching tends to be emotionally restrained.

We tend to think that rhetorical flourish draws too much attention to the personality of the individual preacher and appeals to the emotions of listeners in ways that are not likely to translate into sustained Christian discipleship and maturity. Frequently, sermons narrate some part of the story of God acting in history, so that the congregation is reminded of its true identity through remembering the larger narrative. In general, sermons are important for Mennonites, but probably not as central to their worship as in some other Protestant traditions.

In many congregations, a period of open sharing or reflection typically follows a sermon. Although Christians accustomed to worshipping in high-church traditions may find the sharing time to be uncomfortably personal, for Mennonites this is an important part of worship. Here members of the congregation have the freedom to respond affirmatively to the sermon. Yet they might also elaborate on an underdeveloped idea or even respectfully challenge or question a point presented. The sharing period is also an opportunity for members to inform others of important events in their lives, for which they seek the prayers of the believing community.

Sharing personal details of life—confessions, health-related concerns, stories testifying to God's presence, news about upcoming events—reveals the fabric of the church as a living community. Mennonites believe that these details are appropriately offered in worship because they express a desire to bring all of our lives before God, with no sharp division between the sacred and the secular.

A typical Mennonite worship service would also devote a block of time to Christian education for both children and adults. The Sunday school, sometimes called the nurture hour, is an occasion for more intense Bible study, a focused response to the sermon, or perhaps discussion of a particular issue. Here again, there is a strong emphasis on hearing the voices and perspectives of a wide range of members. Mennonites respect pastoral leadership, but they also assume that discernment of God's will and direction happens in the midst of group reflection and discussion. Members are not merely passive recipients of instruction from a professional clergy.

Woven in and around these formal elements of worship is yet another crucial component of a typical Mennonite service. This is the informal fellowship and conversation that happens before or after the service in the foyer, over coffee in the fellowship hall, on the way to the parking lot, or through contacts with each other by phone or activities during the week.

All of these elements of a typical Sunday morning service contribute to a Mennonite understanding of worship. Mennonites recognize that the Spirit of God finds expression and the resurrected Jesus is incarnated in the body of believers. We encounter God at church as we worship, sing, share, listen, and learn from others.

11
The Visible Church

Practices That Shape Community

Mennonite congregations are created and sustained by shared practices, practices anchored in the decision of the believer to join the church through the ritual of baptism and the regular celebration of worship. But Mennonite congregational life is enriched and deepened by a series of additional practices as well. Although none of these are unique to Anabaptist-Mennonite tradition, each is intwined by a set of biblical and theological convictions that give a distinctive character to the Mennonite understanding of the church.

Communion. Along with the broader Christian tradition, Mennonites consider communion, the Lord's Supper, to be a central practice of the faithful church. The meaning that they bring to this event, however, is rather different from the dominant understandings in the Catholic church and many Protestant traditions. Catholics understand communion to be a sacrament that actually confers divine grace, with the bread and the wine literally becoming the body and blood of Jesus Christ. Mennonites, however, generally speak of communion in more symbolic language. As with baptism, the point here is not to reduce communion to the status of being merely a symbol: communion points to a profound reality of

Christ's living presence in ourselves and in the gathered body of believers. But partaking of the bread and juice themselves is not a mysterious event focused on the careful preparation of the elements or the crucial words of consecration offered by an ordained clergy.

Traditionally, Mennonites have referred to communion as the Lord's Supper, calling attention to the setting in which Jesus first introduced this practice to the disciples. As the Gospels relate the story, Jesus has traveled to Jerusalem in anticipation of a confrontation with Jewish and Roman authorities and his eventual crucifixion. There, shortly before his time of testing and suffering is about to begin, Jesus gathers with his disciples for a final meal where he can remind them once more of the most basic themes of the kingdom of God.

He begins the meal with a surprise. As his tired disciples gather around the table, Jesus adopts the role of the servant of the house and proceeds to wash their dirty feet (John 13). When Peter, often the spokesperson for the disciples, protests—after all, Jesus has just been welcomed into Jerusalem as a heroic leader!—Jesus reminds his disciples that true leaders are servants of others and that the power of love is, paradoxically, revealed in a posture of vulnerability and weakness.

Then he presides over a simple meal, using the occasion to prepare his disciples for the suffering that awaits him and all of his followers who are prepared to follow after him. "When you eat bread," Jesus tells them, "think of my body that is about to suffer. When you drink wine, think of my blood that is going to be shed" (cf. 1 Cor 11:23). The Lord's Supper is thus a collective act of remembering.

Like baptism, participation in the Lord's Supper holds multi-faceted meanings for Mennonites. It is, first and foremost, a reminder of the self-giving love of Jesus and an occasion for members to recall their baptismal vows to follow Christ in daily discipleship. When we eat the bread and drink the cup of communion, we remember that the power of God is revealed in vulnerability and weakness. We anticipate the possibility of suffering. And we remind ourselves that the path Jesus calls us to follow may strip us of our security.

The *Didache*, one of the earliest descriptions of worship practices in the Christian tradition, describes the bread and wine of the Lord's Supper with the metaphor of wheat kernels and grapes. Kernels of wheat must be ground into fine grain and merged with other kernels before they can serve their higher purpose of becoming bread. And grapes must be crushed and mingled with the juice of other grapes before they can become wine. Likewise, Christians must be prepared to relinquish their individual identity so that they might become part of the larger purpose of God's presence in the world. The Anabaptists drew heavily on this image and frequently referred to it in their celebrations of the Lord's Supper.

We do not travel that path alone. The Lord's Supper is also about "re-membering," or reconstituting, the body of Christ—the church. In taking communion the gathered believers are re-forming themselves as the body of Christ. Eating bread and drinking juice is not just an individual experience of private devotion but an occasion for recognizing that God is present in the *community* of fellow believers. It shows that the church is more than just the sum of its individual members.

The unity of the church celebrated at communion is an important part of the church's witness. An older tradition in the Mennonite church regarded communion as an opportunity for careful reflection about the health of relationships among members in the congregation. Recalling the warning of the apostle Paul against "taking communion unworthily" (1 Cor 11:27), ministers would formally inquire of each member whether or not they "were at peace with God and with their fellow believers." If there was enmity or unresolved tensions between members, then they could not participate in communion until those issues were resolved.

Finally, Mennonites also understand communion to be a meal that points toward the culmination of history. This is the great wedding banquet of the Lamb spoken of in Revelation (19), when people from all over the earth will gather together around a table, united by their common confession of the lordship of Christ. This will include rich and poor, men and women, new believers and mature saints, people of all racial, ethnic, and economic groups. Here, in the fullness of time, the unity of creation that God intended for humanity will be completely restored. Here, social hierarchies will be leveled and all Christians will join as equal members of one great family in praise and worship to God. Sharing a simple meal around a common table reminds us that the church is a counter-cultural social reality, made up of imperfect people, to be sure, but living in the anticipation and hope of the new creation that is still to come.

The celebration of the Lord's Supper is therefore a multifaceted event. It reminds us that we *have been saved* in Christ, through his teachings, example, death, and resurrection. It reminds us that *we are being saved*, in the fellowship and support of his living body, the church. And it reminds us that we *will be saved*, as we look forward in hope to the resurrection and the fulfillment of history, when God's new creation will be realized fully "on earth as it is in heaven."

So the practice of communion is indeed a holy moment for Mennonites, not because the elements of the bread and wine that transform us. Rather, communion serves as a dramatic, lived reminder of the larger, all-encompassing reality of God's trans-forming presence in every moment of our life, if we are open to participate with God in that unfolding mystery.

Foot Washing. In a closely related way, the practice of foot washing—of literally washing the feet of other members of the church—gives a concrete embodied expression to these deep understandings about the nature of faith. Foot washing may seem foreign in our culture. But that is precisely what makes it such a powerful symbol. In the intimacy of touching another person's feet, foot washing calls us to an invasion of the privacy so coveted in American culture. In this gesture of intimate familiarity, foot wash-ing reminds us that the church family is larger than, and prior to, our biological family. In the physical posture of humility, foot washing poignantly enacts the leveling of all social, economic, racial, or cultural differences that can easily serve as tools of supe-riority. By anchoring our statements about love and mutual sub-mission in a dramatic gesture of service, foot washing keeps in check our impulses to spiritualize rituals.

Mutual Aid. Although foot washing is a tangible sign of love and mutual submission within the church, the long tradition of mutual aid is an even more concrete expression of these same values. Historically, the practice of sharing material aid to needy congre-gational members was often a practical necessity. In the face of persecution and the upheaval of forced migrations, Anabaptists frequently relied on the support of each other for their very survival. This was certainly the case for the first Hutterites. Forced to flee the city of Nikolsburg, Moravia in the spring of 1528, they pooled all of their belongings on a sheet, in an act of desperation. But the Hutterites would never have made the practice of "community of goods" into a central feature of their faith if there were not also deep biblical and theological reasons to support the principle.

Throughout their history, Mennonites have been keenly aware of Jesus's radical teachings about wealth and his invitation to be freed from slavery to material possessions. After all, Adam and Eve did not own private property before the fall. Ownership of material things, some early Anabaptists argued, is an extension of our ego that reduces our dependence on God and on each other. Christians whose hearts are truly in accord with the spirit of Christ will relin-quish their grasp on possessions and yield themselves—their time, resources, and talents—fully to the community of faith.

The foundation for Anabaptist teaching on mutual aid came from the example of the early church as described in Acts 2 and 4. As the apostolic church emerged in the months following Pentecost, members regularly sold property and freely distributed the proceeds to those within the church who were in need. The seriousness of this imperative to share possessions freely, without reserve, is made clear in the example of Ananias and Sapphira. Their deceitfulness about their qualified generosity (they lied as they kept some of the proceeds of a land sale for themselves) led to their untimely deaths (Acts 5). For Anabaptists, the message of the story was clear: to be selfish is to die, if not physically, then spiritually. Unlike the Hutterites, who made community of goods an essential part of Christian faith, most other Anabaptist groups, including the Mennonites, have taught that mutual aid should be voluntary, with a strong emphasis on generosity and simplicity. Today, many Mennonites participate in a denomination-wide form of mutual aid insurance, and most congregations have a specific fund set aside for members with special financial needs. Equally important, Mennonite congregations are frequently divided into small groups that meet regularly for meals, prayer, or service projects as a way of interacting with members of the congregation beyond the nuclear family. Anyone moving into or out of the community can assume that members of the congregation will be on hand to help with the transition. Frequently, mutual aid takes the form of hospitality, in sharing meals or opening up homes as needs arise. For several decades, a booklet entitled *Mennonite Your Way* has circulated widely. In it individuals register their openness to host travelers in their homes. The practice not only saves travel costs but also provides for an opportunity to meet interesting people and to enjoy the pleasure of extending hospitality to newfound friends.

Behind all of these practices is an understanding of the church as our "first family," in which each member contributes freely of their possessions in response to the needs of other members. At its best, mutual aid is a reminder that we are dependent on God for all that we have. Sharing with others is an expression of thanks to God and a way of valuing the community.

Accountability/Discipline. The practice of mutual aid focuses on the sharing of material possessions. Yet the Anabaptist-Mennonite tradition has understood the mutual obligations of Christian believers to extend beyond possessions. To be a member of the Christian community also implies a readiness to share fully in the care and nurture of souls. The practice expressing this commitment is often called church discipline, though a more descriptive phrase might be mutual accountability.

In our culture today, the language of accountability—or church discipline—nearly always has a negative connotation. It is often associated with punishment or the imposition of the will of the powerful over the behavior of the less powerful. In truth, the practice of church discipline has sometimes been abused in Mennonite settings by overzealous members or power-hungry ministers. But the central principle behind the practice is actually rooted in a profound sense of love and in the pastoral hope of restoring the wayward member to a right relationship with God and with other members of the community.

This more positive connotation of "discipline" is readily evident in secular settings. In sports, for example, the discipline of regular drills and rigorous conditioning make it possible for athletes to compete at their highest level for the duration of the game. A disciplined group, where each player unselfishly contributes in a way that builds up the entire team, is more likely to be successful than a squad that depends on raw individual talent alone. Discipline in a congregational setting is no different.

As with all church practices, Mennonites understand church discipline to be grounded firmly in Scripture. Christ's teaching in Matthew 18 provides both a mandate for discipline as well as helpful instructions regarding an appropriate process. Discipline begins with private conversation and only gradually moves into the more public context of the entire congregation. At each step, the person in question has an opportunity to reflect upon their actions and to explain them. Members recognize the possibility that those who are initiating the discipline might have misunderstood the situation. In any event, excommunication—an extremely rare occurrence in contemporary Mennonite practice—would take place only at the end of a long process. Even then, it is not so much a rejection of the individual as a formal recognition that the person in question is intent on pursuing a direction fundamentally at odds with the commitments and understandings of the group as a whole. These basic principles are affirmed in Paul's writings to the church at Corinth where he admonished the body to unity (1 Cor 12:25-27) and emphasized the separated nature of the faithful church from the fallen world (2 Cor 6:14–7:1).

At times the Anabaptist-Mennonite quest for a church "without stain or wrinkle" (Eph 5:27) has led to unhealthy forms of legalism and perfectionism. Nevertheless, the goal of church discipline is not punitive but restorative. Discipline seeks to shepherd a wayward member to a fuller understanding of faith, discipleship, and relations within the fellowship of believers.

The practice of church discipline is closely interconnected with other distinctive Mennonite convictions, especially those of voluntary baptism and nonviolence. For example, joining the church is a genuinely voluntary commitment to live in accordance with the teachings of the community. Therefore, the integrity of that choice can be preserved only if it is possible for the community to discipline members who, at some later date, began to teach or do things that are at odds with the commitments of the congregation. A church without discipline, as Anabaptists never tired of pointing out, might just as well baptize babies. In their minds, the practice of discipline guaranteed that the voluntary decision to become a member of the church continued to be an *active* choice.

In a related fashion, discipline practiced in accordance with Matthew 18 was also a clear testimony to the nonviolent rule of Christ. In sharp contrast to the state churches, who preserved unity by intimidating, torturing, and executing heretics, the Anabaptists insisted that the conscience could not be swayed by physical force. The biblical model of the ban and shunning was consistent with Christ's teaching of nonviolent, active love.

The Mennonite practice of discipline and the commitment to mutual accountability are never simple matters. They reveal an assumption that the community is constantly prepared to engage in the hard work of discernment, ready to distinguish between essentials and peripherals in the details of everyday faith and practice. Sometimes in the past, a firm commitment to exercise of discipline has become an end in itself, and thus the source of more conflicts than it resolved. But the deeper conviction preserved in the practice of mutual accountability is that we are indeed connected to each other as the body of Christ. How we live as the body of Christ matters in ways that go beyond the personal taste and whim of each individual. At the heart of discipline is a desire to fulfill Christ's prayer for unity in the Gospel of John that the church "may be one" so that "the world may believe" (17:21).

Separation of Church and State

Yet another characteristic practice of the Mennonite church is the conviction that the Christian's allegiance to the church comes before the demands of obedience to the state. For much of the Middle Ages, and indeed well into the eighteenth century, Europeans generally assumed that the church and the state were inextricably fused, usually with the church serving as an arm of the state much like the Department of Education or Commerce. Today, of course, the separation of church and state strikes us as an obvious legal principle, deeply rooted in constitutional law. Even so, its actual implementation continues to be a source of political debate and judicial consideration. Many American Christians, for example, continue to regard the United States as a Christian nation and frequently speak in ways that seem to blur the distinction between allegiance to the nation and allegiance to the church.

In the sixteenth century the Anabaptist tried to define the church as a voluntary association of believers whose first loyalty was to Christ and whose primary identity transcended national boundaries. This effort appeared to be revolutionary and threatening. Mennonites continue this tradition today by holding their citizenship rather lightly. Although they pray regularly for government leaders, obey the laws, and generally pay their taxes, Mennonites are nonetheless quite cautious about the language of nationalism, especially when it takes on a religious tone. For them, the link between the way of Christ and the policies of the nation-state is tenuous at best. Some Mennonites have chosen to engage in the world of politics as an expression of their faith. But most are more comfortable connecting with the world through service and outreach programs, especially in local or international contexts where the church is the primary agent of social change.

Mission: Noncoercive and Invitational

Still another practice central to the identity of the Mennonite church is that of invitation, or mission. Since Mennonites do not assume that everyone in a Christian society is actually a Christian, missions begin close to home, with children, relatives, neighbors, and friends. In the early years of their history, Mennonites had limited access to pulpits or printing presses. So the rapid spread of the movement was due almost entirely to face-to-face contacts, focused initially on family networks, friendship groups, and occupational circles. An itinerant preacher might go to the home of someone sympathetic to the Anabaptists, read and expound on Scripture to the friends and relatives of the household, and baptize those who were ready to commit themselves to the movement.

Eventually, however, persecution blunted the missionary edge of the movement. As a result, European and North American Mennonites in the eighteenth and nineteenth century became known as "the quiet in the land." They were agrarian people who kept largely to themselves and relied primarily on large families for their numerical growth. In the early twentieth century, Mennonites slowly recovered a strong commitment to outreach, albeit with a distinctive style and tone that sets them apart from the more aggressive and visible crusade-style missions of American evangelicals.

Mennonite mission has often taken a variety of forms. As with other Christian groups, Mennonites believe that the invitation to salvation must find expression in words, through preaching, teaching, sharing, witnessing. "Always be prepared," writes Peter, "to give an answer to everyone who asks you to give the reason for the hope that you have" (1 Pet 3:15). But Mennonites have traditionally been somewhat hesitant to think of mission primarily as a set of arguments or ideas that need to be communicated in a persuasive, convincing way. More typically, Mennonites would see their approach to mission as grounded in the lived testimony of an upright, compassionate way of life. Since salvation in the Mennonite understanding is always associated with a changed life—what the New Testament calls a "new creature in Christ"—it is not surprising that wherever they went, Mennonites quickly gained the reputation of being honest and trustworthy—a fact that authorities alternatively admired or resented.

At stake in mission is the integrity of the message: a witness to Christ is credible only if actions are aligned with words. "No one has ever seen God," we read in 1 John 4:12; "but if we love each other, God lives in us and his love is made complete in us." In other words, God becomes visible in the world through the example of Christians who love one another.

All of these forms of mission—preaching, the witness of a consistent moral life, and the practices of the gathered community—are essential expressions of Mennonite outreach.

Summary

Mennonites envision the church as a community of voluntary Christian believers. Their determination to follow the costly teachings of Christ leads them inevitably to a tension with the world. This gathered community, at least in its ideal form, provides a communal context for reading and discerning the meaning of Scripture. It is this gathered community that nurtures the new convert in the faith, sustaining, challenging, and disciplining the disciple in the high calling of following the way of Christ. It is this gathered community—not the state, nor the institutional church, nor the family, nor the self—that is the primary focus of God's saving acts in history.

It might be helpful to think of a Mennonite understanding of the church as analogous to a family. There are abstract legal definitions of families, of course, but most people think of families as a group of people whose lives intersect with each other frequently and at many different levels. There are the routines of daily life—

eating, cleaning, washing, coordinating schedules. There are the occasional squabbles and disagreements. There are the moments of pure joy—of intimacy and absolute trust.

All of these practices, these many overlapping interactions, together constitute a family. A family's identity can never be reduced to any single moment or event. Instead, it becomes a precious gift through the many interactions of individual members who come to recognize that their own individual identity is incomplete apart from the commitments and practices of the larger family.

The strong emphasis on the church as a community whose identity is distinct from the world around it could give the impression that the Mennonite church is in danger of becoming a cult. Such a group controls the decisions of individuals so tightly that personal identity and freedom disappear altogether. While it is true that a Mennonite understanding of Christian faith does challenge the individualism of our culture, the goal is not to destroy distinct personalities, but to enable authentic individual identity to flourish by building up the body of Christ in a way that honors the dignity of each person.

Despite all of these high ideals, Mennonites do not escape the basic power struggles and inequities that are part of the fallen world. Sometimes in our congregations people with the loudest voices shape the agenda. Sometimes the people who contribute most to the budget wield a disproportionate amount of influence. Sometimes the opinions of educated professionals drown out the voices of blue-collar workers. And sometimes the perspectives of white males dominate. Clearly, Mennonite churches are not perfect. Yet within the Mennonite tradition one can find many resources to challenge the misuse of power and to call the congregation toward a higher standard.

At their best, Mennonite congregations are settings for Christian practice that bear consistent and joyful witness to God's love for the world and God's desire that all people live in respect and trust for each other.

12

The Visible Church

A Critique... and Ongoing Questions

For many modern readers, the Mennonite understanding of the church may not sound all that radical. After all, the principle of church-state separation has been a cornerstone of the U.S. Constitution for more than two centuries. And in a secular culture, where religious beliefs are often dismissed as harmless private mythologies, Christians across the denominational spectrum have grown accustomed to thinking of their churches as voluntary associations, sustained only by the active choices of adult, committed believers.

In the sixteenth century, however, the Anabaptist view of the church triggered a violent reaction. The idea of a voluntary church—which individuals were free to accept or reject—seemed to challenge the timeless unity of the Catholic church and threatened the stability of the political order. Moreover, the argument that all of life, including politics and economics, should be judged according to the standard of the New Testament, drove a wedge into the fusion of Christianity and culture that had defined Christendom for more than a millennium.

Not surprisingly, the political and religious authorities of the day, Catholic and Protestant alike, denounced the Anabaptists as anarchists who were destroying the foundations of European society. Today, thankfully, no one is advocating the death penalty for Mennonites. But the concerns expressed in the sixteenth century helpfully illuminate several key theological issues that remain points of continuing debate between Mennonites and other Christian denominations still today.

The Mennonite Understanding of Church and State Is Irresponsible

The Mennonite reluctance to swear oaths, to participate in the police force or to serve in the military seems to undermine the very basis of civil government. If everyone would take this position, their opponents charge, then society would be completely vulnerable to criminals from within and attacks from terrorists and neighboring states from without. Clearly, someone needs to assume the responsibility of preserving order in human society. Not to do so, the argument goes, means that the weakest members of society, precisely those who are most in need of Christian charity, will inevitably become victims of tyranny and oppression. The Mennonite understanding of church and state is simply irresponsible.

The Mennonite response to this, though not always convincing to their opponents, has generally taken the following form:

1. We believe that Christians in all countries should respect those in political authority. Christians should pray for their leaders, and that they should obey the laws of the land, as long as they do not conflict with the teachings of Jesus. Mennonites have never been advocates of anarchy or revolution against established political authorities. Instead, as we have seen in an earlier chapter, most Mennonites acknowledge that the state is an ordering of God that has a positive role in protecting the good and punishing evildoers. In a fallen world, order is better than anarchy. Christians, in accordance with Romans 13, should generally support the state as it carries out this important, though limited, role. In the Romans 13 passage, however, Paul describes a state whose leaders were not understood to be Christians. And even though order is preferable to chaos, it does not follow from this passage that it is *Christians* who are obliged to use violence to bring about this order. Instead, Paul instructs Christians in the preceding chapter to remember that they are first and foremost citizens of a different kingdom: "Do not conform any longer to the pattern of this world" (12:2). "Bless those who persecute you" (12:14). "Do not repay anyone evil for evil" (12:17). "Do not take revenge" (12:19). In short, writes Paul, "Do not be overcome by evil, but overcome evil with good" (12:21).

2. In a related vein, Mennonites have made it clear that they do share a sense of responsibility for the poor, weak, and powerless in society. Though they have not always practiced this consistently, most Mennonites would argue they are not fleeing from responsibility on behalf of victims of violence. Instead, we have readily responded to human suffering with "a cup of cold water" offered in the name of Christ (cf. Matt 10:42). Mennonites are often disproportionately represented in service vocations, especially in areas such as teaching, social work, and the medical professions. Mennonite Disaster Service frequently coordinates the efforts of hundreds of volunteers to help families clean up and rebuild communities destroyed by natural disasters. The Victim-Offender Reconciliation Program (VORP), founded by Mennonites and based on the principle of restoration rather than retribution, offers a creative alternative to the criminal justice system. And the Mennonite commitment to expressing Christ's love beyond national boundaries has found consistent expression in the Mennonite Central Committee, a relief and service agency with grassroots development programs around the world. To be sure, Mennonites are far from perfect in carrying out these goals. But inconsistencies in the Mennonite witness are no reason for Christians to cease in their efforts to put the teachings of Jesus into practice in daily life.

3. Finally, Mennonites have raised thoughtful questions about the assumed effectiveness of violence as a responsible means of pre-

serving social order. Many of us have grown accustomed to thinking that the sanctioned violence of the state (through its police force and army) is an absolute necessity for an orderly life. Yet, we are often far less willing to count the actual long-term costs—financially, emotionally, and spiritually—that the use of state violence exacts from its citizens. With numbing frequency, violence (even in the service of a righteous cause) leads to more violence. At the very least, those advocating the use of lethal violence to guarantee order and security should be held to a closer accounting regarding the effectiveness of this solution.

The Mennonite View of the Church and Society Is Too Dualistic

In a similar way, many critics of the Mennonites' tradition have suggested that their understanding of the church is excessively dualistic. By describing reality in terms of the gathered church that is visibly separate from the fallen world, Mennonites seem to promote a worldview with sharply polarized extremes in a way that sounds naive, arrogant, and maybe even dangerous. Either one is part of the redeemed community of saints, Mennonites seem to be saying, or one is part of the fallen order of the world. Such a dualistic perspective seems to suggest that only a few people (the Mennonites?) are God's "chosen people," while the rest of the world somehow lies outside of God's favor. In its worst form, the Mennonite understanding of the two kingdoms could promote a cultlike view of the church as a haven of security amid a world going to hell, with all of the potential for spiritual and emotional abuse that goes along with such absolutist claims.

Although few contemporary Mennonites would describe their congregation in such dualistic language, the critique is worth taking seriously, especially since it suggests that Mennonites believe all those who are outside the Mennonite fold are somehow damned to hell.

A Mennonite response to these criticisms may begin by simply recognizing the fact that all people—Christians and non-Christians alike—make ethical choices. Human beings are constantly making value judgments that affect our lives and the lives of those around us. Such choices of opting for "this" instead of "that" inevitably imply that we are making a *judgment* against the alternative. So if the Christian effort to respond faithfully to God's call means that our action is somehow judging those who make other choices, then Mennonites must plead "guilty as charged." There is, however, no possible way around this dilemma if moral choices are to have any meaning at all.

So part of the charge is true. Mennonites do indeed have a vision of the church that is sometimes in tension with other established understandings. But they pursue that vision, not with the intention of condemning others, but to remain faithful to their understanding of the teachings of Jesus.

In a related vein, Mennonites have always regarded humility as a cardinal virtue. Throughout their history they have sought to speak their convictions with clarity and to abide by the teachings of Jesus as they best know how to do. But they do not claim to have grasped the Truth completely and fully. The desire is always to be attentive to Scripture and the movement of the Holy Spirit within a community that is actively testing and discerning the will of God.

So even if the Mennonite understanding of the church suggests a sharp line between the church and the world, Mennonites do not assume that this line needs to be defended with lethal force. The Truth is always bigger than our arguments or own weapons. We seek to reflect the Truth without fear; but we will not impose the Truth on any others against their will.

Do Mennonites think that members of other denominations are Christians? Yes! Mennonites are very reluctant to declare a judgment about the salvation of other people. This, thankfully, is for God to decide, not humans. Within our limited understanding and fallible natures, we are called to make discerning choices regarding beliefs and practices. But we do so knowing that our understandings in the past have sometimes been incomplete or even wrong. This acknowledgment does not lead to relativism, but to constant caution about how absolute we can be in our ultimate judgments. Mennonites believe that all of us are accountable to God—that we all will need to stand before our Creator. Ultimate judgment, however, remains in God's hands alone. It is not up to us to determine the salvation of anyone, least of all others who also claim the name of Christ.

So Mennonites plead a kind of cautious ignorance on this question. We live in gratitude for God's gift of grace to us. This grace calls us to reject the lies of the world and empowers us to mold our lives every day into the image of Christ. But at the same time, Mennonites are hesitant about claiming to know more than what we are given to know.

Ongoing Questions Among Contemporary Mennonites

1. What Are Appropriate Forms of Worship? Few topics are likely more relevant—and potentially more divisive—within the Mennonite church today than the question of worship style, especially when it comes to music. Part of the energy behind the discussion stems from the fact that, over time, patterns and forms of worship can easily come to be almost indistinguishable from worship itself. Few Catholics, for example, would insist that the communion wine absolutely has to be served in a silver chalice. But most would find it unsettling, if not outright offensive, for a priest to suddenly start serving communion in a Dixie cup. The architecture of our church buildings, the order of events in our worship hour, the aesthetic decor of our meeting spaces, the use (or nonuse) of technology in worship, and perhaps especially the texts, rhythms, and forms of our music—all these considerations are ultimately extrinsic to God, the ultimate object of our worship. But we grow deeply attached to these details, so that it often becomes quite difficult to separate form and substance in our worship.

If there is one distinctive aspect of North American Mennonite worship, it would be the singing, and more specifically, the tradition of four-part singing. For many traditional Mennonite congregations, singing of hymns is one of the few expressions of genuine aesthetic exuberance in the worship experience. It is precisely because hymn singing has been so central to Mennonite worship that the recent introduction in many congregations of a worship band and the accompanying praise music—usually projected onto a screen to free hands for clapping—has become so controversial.

Proponents of praise music often describe it as freeing, as more expressive and heartfelt than conventional hymns. Praise music encourages more movement and energy; to many worshippers, it seems more spiritual. Opponents, on the other hand, complain that praise music turns the worship band into microphoned performers who drown out the congregation, and that the repetitive nature of the choruses reduces Christian theology to a series of simpleminded phrases. Furthermore, critics charge, the lyrics of praise music tend to be highly individualistic in their emphasis on emotions and a personal relationship with Jesus. As such, praise music seems to be introducing into Mennonite worship life a language and form in tension with a tradition that has long emphasized daily discipleship and a prominent role for the community.

Other recent changes in Mennonite worship life have also created congregational tensions. These include a more widespread use of the lectionary as a way of structuring worship themes, more attention to the liturgical year (especially seasons of Advent and Lent), greater appreciation for the role of visual art in worship, and a conscious integration of music from other cultures.

Concerns about innovations in worship are absolutely appropriate. After all, the content and form of our worship shapes us, even as it proclaims our identity to the world around us. Still, it is important to keep such debates in a healthy perspective. One gift of the global Mennonite church has been the reminder of the wide variety of worship practices in other countries and cultures. Moreover, historians know that today's tradition was yesterday's innovation. So even as healthy congregations should be thoughtful about introducing changes, they should also be hesitant to reject new forms of worship outright simply because they do not conform to current habits and tastes.

2. Do Congregations Actually Practice Church Discipline Today? Here again, it is difficult to generalize. In the past the range of issues that Mennonite congregations considered within the purview of the church was remarkably broad: borrowing money, the resolution of inheritance disputes, questions regarding appropriate dress (with the standard ranging from simplicity to conformity), acceptable styles of the prayer (or devotional) covering for women (1 Cor 11:1–16), regulations governing musical instruments, Sunday activities, membership in secret societies (2 Cor 6:14), participation in worldly amusements, or engagement in local politics. Typically, the moment of truth occurred just before communion, when ministers would meet individually with each member to clarify whether or not they were in conformity with the standards of the congregation.

Today, however, congregations are far less clear about the meaning and importance of mutual accountability and less likely to enforce specific teachings of the church through the regular exercise of church discipline. Many older Mennonites carry with them extremely negative memories of the way church discipline had been practiced in their youth. In their experience, discipline was often reserved for a specific set of public sins, often sexual in nature, thus leaving many other sins (economic, attitudinal) to go unchallenged. Moreover, discipline often seemed punitive in nature, or it was carried out in an inconsistent fashion, often by individual ministers who seemed to wield church discipline as a form of personal power.

In reaction to these negative experiences, recent Mennonite practice has been to drop the exercise of church discipline altogether. If discipline exists in Mennonite congregations at all today, it generally assumes an indirect and informal nature. Sermons about pacifism, for example, have the effect of discouraging people who are active in the armed forces from seeking membership. If the church sides with one party of a divorced couple, the other spouse is likely to leave the congregation. Negative messages regarding smoking make it unlikely that a member will light up a cigarette in the church parking lot.

Some see this as a healthy sign that our congregations are more caring, compassionate, and accepting than in earlier generations. Others, however, worry that we are simply accommodating to the pervasive individualism of modern culture. As a sense of shared ethical clarity erodes, they argue, the character of the gathered and visible community that has been so central to Mennonite identity in the past will also be lost.

3. What Is the Relationship of the Congregation to the Denomination? For reasons both historical and theological, Mennonites have generally preferred a congregational form of church governance, though periods of persecution and harassment have reinforced a strong sense of denominational identity. In contrast to the organizational hierarchy of the Catholic, Mennonites do not have a highly developed episcopacy linking the authority of the local pastor to a bishop, archbishop, or pope. Instead, the primary context for reading and interpreting Scripture tends to reside in the face-to-face relationships of the local congregation.

At the same time, Mennonite congregations have almost always developed associations with other like-minded congregations to form conferences (or districts or fellowships). These conferences tended to emerge first around shared understandings of specific ethical concerns related to practices such as nonresistance, mutual aid, or church discipline. Over time, some of these associations began to give more attention to doctrinal matters, so that shared confessions of faith became the glue helping to unite a cluster of congregations.

These regional associations are not always permanent—individual congregations can join or leave them, depending on the circumstances of local leadership and shifting priorities within the congregations. But they serve as a broader forum of discernment, offering pastoral support to congregational leaders, assisting congregations in the selection of pastors, providing shared standards for new ministers, serving as intermediaries in local conflicts, coordinating mission and service efforts, and pooling resources in support of parachurch organizations such as church camps, schools, and historical societies.

Conferences also serve an important function in helping congregations relate to the larger Mennonite denomination. For example, the Mennonite Church USA and Mennonite Church Canada are comprised of regional and provincial conferences and districts. These conferences are represented at the national level through regular leadership consultations and through representatives at denominational conventions. Overseeing the daily work of the denomination are staff who report to an executive board.

In general, the denominational offices give broad oversight to the collective work of the church. A church life and Christian formation board oversees issues of worship, leadership, youth and congregational nurture. A publishing network coordinates church-related publications such as Sunday school curricula, along with church periodicals and books. A witness and mission network oversees a wide range of mission and service programs both in North American and internationally. An education group provides services for dozens of Mennonite elementary schools, high schools, colleges, and seminaries. And a mutual aid organization promotes stewardship education and offers a variety of insurance plans and financial services. In addition to overseeing several specific initiatives (historical, peace and justice, interchurch relations), the denomination has also taken initiative in the formulation of the church's most recent doctrinal statements ("Confession of Faith in a Mennonite Perspective," ratified in 1995).

At the congregational level, Mennonites do not all agree about the relevance of these denominational services or just how the congregation should relate to the broader church body. A tradition wary of a top-down, or hierarchical, approach places high value on free association. Some insist on the virtual autonomy of the congregation, arguing that decisions made at the local level about specific practices (regarding homosexuality, for example) should be respected by conference and denominational leaders even if those decisions are at odds with the official teachings of the larger body. Some congregations have resisted efforts by conferences to screen pastors on matters of their theological training and support for Anabaptist-Mennonite convictions. And some have chaffed at the cultural divide that sometimes separates administrators and ministers in central offices from farmers, merchants, and entrepreneurs in the heartland.

Other Mennonites, by contrast, call attention to the way in which denomination-wide institutions have provided essential services to congregations. Education, missions, service, stewardship, and publications all require resources and collaboration far beyond the level that congregations would be able to provide on their own. Conferences and denominational structures provide a sort of ballast for congregations in times of local conflict or national crisis. They help to restrain the cultural impulse toward fragmentation and localism, enabling congregations to stay in conversation with each other and with the global church.

4. Isn't It Presumptuous to Think of the Church Primarily in Terms of One's Own Denomination or Local Congregation?
Approximately 2 billion people of the world's population currently identify themselves as Christians. Given that only a tiny fraction of this number (1.2 million) are Mennonites, it may seem more than a little arrogant to assume that our understanding of the Christian faith is somehow closer to the truth than 99 percent of the other people who also call themselves Christians.

A significant minority of contemporary Mennonites tend to be quite skeptical about denominational labels and try to minimize their association with the term Mennonite as much as possible. The primary task of Christians, they argue, is to bring the good news of salvation to a lost world. And in carrying out that calling, our message should be focused on Jesus Christ, not on the details of denominational distinctives. These Mennonites are often embarrassed by the legalistic restrictions of an early generation or troubled by the way the traditional Mennonite emphasis on peacemaking has seemed like a hindrance to mission. For them, the denominational label is a historical accident and more likely a burden to be borne than a trademark to be claimed with distinction. If Christians around the world read the same Scriptures, worship the same God, and follow the same Lord, why not simply agree on a few, simple basic truths and become a nondenominational church?

Others, in contrast, have worked vigorously to preserve and enliven a distinctive Mennonite identity, especially in the face of a broad decline in denominational loyalties more generally. In the past, for example, Mennonites did not join the National Council of Churches, the National Association of Evangelicals, or the World Council of Churches. In part, this was because the Mennonite commitment to the gospel of peace made it difficult to enter into close communion with other denominations that defended the just-war tradition. But it also was out of a concern that Mennonites would simply be swallowed up by the sheer numbers of the larger groups.

In the years following World War I, Mennonites began to work closely with the so-called Historic Peace Churches (Quakers, Brethren in Christ, Church of the Brethren) on issues surrounding military conscription and alternative service. This association was further strengthened in the last half of the twentieth century by regular conferences to discuss points of shared theological interest.

In other settings, Mennonites have sought to preserve a distinctive identity while entering vigorously into cooperative ecumenical projects. The relief and service efforts of Mennonite Central Committee, for example, have frequently brought volunteers into close cooperation with workers from other denominations. Mennonite Disaster Service regularly collaborates with their counterparts from other traditions. And Mennonite Mutual Aid has embraced a broad range of denominations in their efforts to provide insurance and financial services within an Anabaptist-Mennonite context.

In recent years, Mennonites have been invited by denominations as diverse as Catholic, Baptist, Reformed, and Lutheran to participate in interchurch dialogues about our understandings of Christian faith and practice. At a more local level, many Mennonite congregations join with other area churches for Thanksgiving, Christmas, or Lenten services. They support each other in local service efforts (Habitat for Humanity, Interfaith Hospitality Network, and so on). They are generally open to giving and receiving communion at each others' worship services. And their pastors often enjoy cordial relations in local ministerial groups. So the boundaries separating the Mennonite church from other Christian traditions are certainly not insurmountable.

On these and other questions, Mennonites are clearly not of one mind. At some basic level, we recognize our fundamental unity with other Christian groups—a unity of faith and worship that transcends our historical and theological distinctions. At the same time, Mennonites are inclined to caution when Christians suggest that the experience of salvation is somehow separate from the concrete practices of the Christian church. For Mennonites, discipleship and the gospel of peace are not accessories to the good news of salvation; they are integral parts of salvation. So we live with a certain tension between our sense of fellowship with other Christians and our awareness of a distinctive identity.

It may be helpful to think of Christian denominations as a kind of family tree. The various branches of an extended family often have their own distinguishing character traits. Yet, to the extent that each branch shares the same trunk and the same roots, each part of the family tree bears a resemblance to the other. Each part is dependent for its very life on a common foundation. For each of us, the primary concern should not be the health of all the other branches, but rather the question that Jesus posed to his disciples: Is our branch bearing fruit? (John 15:2).

13

An Invitation

Mennonites in the (post) Modern World

*I keep asking that the God of our Lord Jesus Christ,
the glorious Father, may give you the Spirit of wisdom
and revelation, so that you may know him better.
I pray also that the eyes of your heart may be enlightened
in order that you may know the hope
to which he has called you.*

—Ephesians 1:16-19

In March of 2004 moviegoers flocked to Mel Gibson's *The Passion of the Christ* in stunning numbers, making this overtly religious film, a dramatic depiction of Christ's final hours, the number one movie in America for four straight weeks. Within six months, the movie grossed nearly 400 million dollars. Acknowledging the movie's success, secular news magazines suddenly began to feature stories about the role of Christian faith in the lives of ordinary people, and Hollywood producers were forced to rethink their traditional bias against religious themes. At about the same time, Rick Warren's *The Purpose-Driven Life* and its sequel, *The Purpose-*

Driven Church, sold millions of copies, dominating secular best-seller lists and setting new records for Christian book sales. Clearly, Christian faith has a firm foothold in the public culture of the United States. When my Japanese seating partner—the marketing researcher who was trying to understand American consumers—asked me to explain what it means to be a Christian, he knew that something important was at stake.

This book has attempted to respond to his question by summarizing some of the basic principles of Christian belief from the perspective of the Anabaptist-Mennonite tradition. I have tried to give a balanced account of the Christian faith, acknowledging that not all Christians agree with the Mennonite perspective. I have also explained several issues of faith and practice about which Mennonites themselves have sometimes differed. Along the way, I have suggested that Christian faith is best understood not as set of doctrines or membership in an institution. Instead, we see it as a fundamentally new way of life, a life that is transformed by a relationship with God, sustained by the support of a loving community, and modeled after the teaching and example of Jesus.

In our brief conversation in the plane, the primary focus of my friend's question was *what* Christians believe. But underneath that curiosity was an even deeper and more profound question: *Why* do Christians believe what they do? A religious worldview might be understandable for people long ago, in Bible times, perhaps, or maybe during the Middle Ages. But why would modern people—educated Westerners in a high-tech, rational, and sophisticated society—continue to trouble themselves with the teachings of an itinerant Jewish carpenter who lived two thousand years ago in a tiny country on the eastern edge of the Mediterranean Sea? Why would people today continue to regard this faith as a plausible way of making sense of the world? Why be a Christian at all?

Even though he did not pose the question quite in that way, I think that this is what my Japanese friend really wanted to know. And it is a fair question. After all, in the modern marketplace of ideas, where the options of consumerism, hedonism, or atheism present themselves with the aggressive self-confidence once reserved for Christianity alone, Christian believers should be prepared to give an account not only of *what* they believe, but *why* they believe it.

In this concluding chapter, what follows is a brief response to that question, . . . along with an invitation.

Life in the Gap

The phone call came on a gray day in February. My youngest brother, then in his first year of medical school, had been experiencing sharp pains in his shoulder and hip. A visit to the doctor turned up nothing, but the pains persisted. So he went to a specialist. There, after a series of complicated tests, the diagnosis became clear: a rapidly growing cancer had metastasized to his bones. He had six to twelve months to live.

With that news, the whole world suddenly seemed to turn upside down. This was not fair! Steve was supposed to have a full life ahead of him. Cancer was an old person's illness, not a disease for a twenty-four-year-old who ate the right foods and exercised regularly. Moreover, Steve was such a good person—gentle, sensitive, and caring. He had spent the previous year volunteering at a low-income clinic and was eager to use his medical skills in service to others. Why would such a promising life be cut short so prematurely?

Perhaps worst of all was the pain—the persistent piercing physical agony that accompanied the cancer's spread through his joints and up his spine. Why should anyone, let alone a young person in the prime of his life, have to endure that much suffering?

Suffering is always personal. But even if we rarely are forced to confront it so dramatically, the pain that accompanied Steve's disappointment and his journey toward death is shared daily, in some small way, by every single human being. Somewhere deep down, we are always aware that the world is badly askew—that there is a stubborn and persistent gap between the world as it *is* and the world as it *ought to be.*

Our awareness of this gap starts almost from the moment of birth. The piercing wail of the newborn suddenly separated from the warmth of the womb, the frustrated cry of a hungry baby, or the late-night terrors of a frightened child—all these are early hints that the world as we experience it is somehow out of joint. That awareness deepens as we grow older. When we notice that a bicycle has disappeared from our front porch, or discover that a local cemetery has been vandalized, or read of another case of child abuse, we are jolted anew with a sense of outrage and disappointment. This is not the way things are supposed to be! When we hear that a teenager has been killed by a drunk driver in a car accident, or that fire has destroyed the home of a poor family, or that a person in church whom you had respected has been caught embezzling funds, we cannot help but think that the world should be more happy, more secure, more predictable, more pain-free than it actually is.

To be human is to walk a continuous tightrope between hope and frustration. We yearn for some larger sense of meaning and purpose to the events in our lives, stubbornly expecting that tomorrow will be better than today. Yet at the same time, we also live in the persistent awareness of past disappointments, fearing that the chasm between hope and reality can never be bridged. Even though we are all taught somewhere along the way that life isn't fair, we can never quite make our peace with the fact that, like Steve, we are always living in the shadow of our own death. Deep down we know that we are living on borrowed time. Each day brings us closer to the moment of our death. And we worry, sometimes desperately, that our one precious life will end unfulfilled, without meaning or purpose.

The challenge before us, perhaps the only challenge that really matters, is to figure out how to live in this precarious balance between persistent hope and our daily experience of disappointment. Each person does this differently, of course. But throughout history people seem to have consistently pursued three main alternatives. Each of these responses is understandable in light of our fear of death and our continuing experience of life's frustrations.

Yet, from the perspective of a Christian, each of these options ultimately turns out to be unsatisfying. If you recognize yourself in one of the descriptions that follows, I hope you will give serious consideration to my suggestion that Christianity offers a response to the human condition that is more authentic, more coherent, and more joyful than the options given to us by our culture. The invitation to Christianity is an invitation to life—a life lived to the fullest.

The Invitation: Truth-Telling in a Culture of Illusions

Faced with the gap between what *is* and what *ought to be*, many people today try to bridge the chasm by pursuing a life of pleasure. "Seize the day," the motto goes. "Eat, drink and be merry, for tomorrow we may die!" By indulging ourselves in every sort of pleasure, we hope to erase, or at least blur, the gap between desire and fulfillment. Some seek the physical pleasure of food or alcohol or drugs. Others try to lose themselves in the sensory thrills of extreme sports or promiscuous sex. Still others give themselves over to the materialistic pleasures of recreational shopping or the challenges of beating the stock market.

This deep craving for pleasure has not gone unnoticed by marketing experts. According to a recent study, the average American sees or hears nearly three thousand advertising messages a day. Jumping out at us from billboards, on television, at the gas pump, in our mail, on the Internet, and at every store, the appeals all communicate the same basic message: Your life is incomplete unless you have this product. You cannot be fully alive or healthy until you wear this name brand. You will have more friends, more fun, more sex, and more happiness if you buy what we are offering.

These messages are remarkably powerful. But they are nearly always lies. They are deceptions, feeding on our deep sense of insecurity and our readiness to buy into the illusion that physical pleasure or the accumulation of things will bring us joy. Yet, deep down, all of us know that the pleasures of the body are not the same as happiness. And we know from experience that our appetite for pleasure can never be fully satisfied. No drug-induced high, adrenaline rush, or euphoric shopping spree will ever finally appease our desire for still more pleasure, or satisfy the craving that we have for a deeper sense of meaning and purpose in life.

In a society full of such illusions, Christian faith offers the possibility of telling the truth. With remarkable insight, the biblical story captures both the anguish and the hopes of our human condition. And it invites us to see beneath the surface, to step out of crazy-mirror appearances of our culture, to a life that is authentic and honest.

Christians believe that we were created by a God who loves us, who has designed us for a purpose and intended for us to live in trust and intimacy with each other. We are loved not because of anything we do, or what we wear, or for our talents. Instead, we are loved simply because God chose to love us.

The fact that God loves us fully and completely, without any conditions, is good news indeed, news that frees us from the world of illusions. Jesus understood the liberating power of this message. He was not afraid, for example, to tell the rich young ruler—a man of great power and wealth, and a potential supporter of his cause— that he needed to let go of his money (cf. Matt 19; Luke 18). Jesus did not hesitate to publicly challenge the Pharisees who conscientiously paid tithes on mint leaves while ignoring basic questions of justice. And he dared to openly associate with people who had no respect or power—such as tax collectors and sinners, diseased people and children—recognizing in them the image of God.

At the same time, Christians know that human beings are not perfect. Christians fully recognize the human tendency toward egotism and pride, and they name this reality for what it really is: sin. Sin has disrupted the goodness of God's created order, poisoning our relationships with each other and with God. Repeatedly, we make choices that go against our own best interest, acting as though we, not God, were masters of our destiny. Sickness, pain, and suffering are all consequences of a sinful, fallen world. To be a Christian is to acknowledge both sides of this reality. A loving God has created us for a purpose. Yet we are also deeply flawed, prone to selfishness, and in need of redemption.

In the midst of this tension, Christian faith offers a language for speaking truthfully about the world. It names things for what they are, while at the same time calling us to embrace the image of God within us that pulls us toward a life of hope and wholeness. Christian faith is an invitation to live truthfully. We are broken and flawed people living in a broken and flawed world. Yet precisely because God's love for us is unconditional, we can be honest about our shortcomings. Nothing exposed to the light is so bad that it will jeopardize God's love. This awareness frees us from the frantic pursuit of pleasure and allows us to live authentically.

To live in truth is not always easy. Accepting God's love, and molding your life in the light of that love, will invariably run against the grain of our culture and challenge the status quo. But the freedom of being truly transparent, open, honest to the world is good news. It will make you come alive!

"You will know the truth," Jesus promised, "and the truth will make you free!" (John 8:32).

The Invitation: Coherence and Community in a Culture of Cynicism

If some people try to bridge the gap between hope and disappointment by pursuing pleasure, others respond to the tension by giving up altogether. Faced with enough disappointments, some people conclude that life, like the gambling tables in Las Vegas, is simply rigged against us. Since it is impossible to make sense out of the many disappointments that come our way, intelligent people eventually learn to abandon the struggle for meaning. They resign themselves to the fact that life is an arbitrary flow of events over which they have little control and they become cynics.

For the cynic, all expressions of hope are illusions, betraying an ignorance or sentimentalism that simply will not stand up to the cold facts of reality. The cynic's path is usually a lonely retreat into a private understanding of truth. Any talk about broader ideals, or the common good, or sacrifice on behalf of others must be naive or self-serving. And so we start to live fragmented lives, cut off from each other, intent only on defending our self-interests in a private, small, and lonely world.

In the midst of this culture of cynicism, Christian faith offers the possibility of a coherent and centered life, a life energized by hope and sustained by the support of a broader community. The Christian life is coherent because its foundation is grounded in a God bigger than the self or the culture around us. Christians believe that God created each of us for a purpose, and that God invites each of us to live in a relationship of trust and love. This is no guarantee that every moment of our lives will be free from pain or disappointment. Indeed, Jesus's life of compassion eventually led to a painful crucifixion and his death. But it does mean that a commitment to embodying God's love to others will reveal a pattern of meaning and direction in life that runs deeper than the frustration of the moment. The larger story of the Gospels is that death does not have the final word. Christians live in the conviction that life will ultimately triumph over death, that service to others is the antidote to despair, and that love is a force more powerful than fear.

Moreover, Christ becomes visible in the world today in the form of the Christian community. In the fellowship of other believers, Christians celebrate God's living presence through worship, singing, prayer, and sharing. In their gathering, Christians re-center themselves in a God who is the ground of all being, the unmoving pivot around which all of life revolves, bringing order and coherence to our fragmented lives. The Christian community reminds us that we are surrounded by friends who truly care about us and make visible God's love for us and God's care for the world. Christians believe that in the community of believers you will discover a way of life that is more coherent, more authentic, and more joyful than the cynicism of our culture.

The Invitation: Forgiveness and Love in a Culture of Violence

If pleasure-seeking and cynicism hold a powerful appeal for many people, still others are convinced that the gap between our desires and their fulfillment will be resolved only by resorting to coercion and violence: the raw power of a gun, the blunt force of a fist, or the physical or emotional abuse of a vulnerable person. By exercising coercive power, we create the impression, if only temporarily, that we can reshape reality according to our own wishes. Violence offers the fleeting illusion that we can transcend our own mortality. It allows us to think that we are actually in control of our lives—that we can guarantee the outcome of our desires by bending the will of those around us to our command.

Like the pursuit of pleasure or the lonely fog of cynicism, the intoxicating logic of power is deeply embedded within our cultural reality. Indeed, encounters with violence—either personally or vicariously—are so commonplace that they no longer shock or even surprise us. Another bomb explodes in Jerusalem, Kabul, or Baghdad leaving behind the charred remains of a bus or market-place, a host of weeping bystanders, and bloodstained sheets covering the bodies of the victims. A popular TV series featuring forensic investigators re-creates in graphic detail a murder in which a young woman is decapitated. A prime-time reality show with live cameras offers us footage of real-life police chases, filled with dramatic car wrecks, beatings, and shootouts. According to the National Institute on Media and the Family, by the time an average child leaves elementary school, he or she will have witnessed 8,000 murders on television alone. That figure will rise to 40,000 by their eighteenth birthday, in addition to nearly 200,000 additional acts of violence.

Experts have long debated whether prolonged visual exposure to violence inclines viewers to become more violent themselves. But there can be little doubt that the cumulative effect of a culture saturated with violence is a gradual numbing process. After watching fifty people killed in the latest Hollywood thriller, the fifty-first murder no longer seems so shocking. Slowly, the message insinuates itself into our most basic assumptions about life: violence is normal; violence is simply the way the world works, the way people resolve their problems. When circumstances do not line up with my expectations, the obvious solution is to bring the world into alignment by using force.

Since our causes are just and we are good people, we naturally assume that our use of violence will always be restrained, responsible, and righteous. After all, we are fighting on the side of Truth, keeping the forces of Evil at bay. But like the seductions of pleasure and cynicism, the impulse to pursue our desires through violence turns out to be only another version of despair. It may close the gap of our frustration momentarily, but no act of coercive power is without consequences. Using force to impose order on the world always generates a violent response, so that violence inevitably gives birth to more violence. The "smart bombs" intended to win the war on terrorism sow the seeds for still more retribution. They nourish the hatreds of another generation of righteous warriors determined to avenge the memories of their dead children. The fear and resentment triggered by violence erode the foundations of the peace that the "righteous" use of force promises to bring, so that at some basic level the world turns out to be just as "out of joint" as before.

In the midst of a culture drunk on the twisted logic of violence, Christian faith invites you to a life of compassion, forgiveness, and love. God has loved us and forgiven us while we were still sinners— indeed, while we were yet enemies of God. Therefore, Christians extend that love to others by letting go of their human desire for vengeance and retribution against others, including those who might be considered our enemies. At the foundation of the Christian faith is the life and example of Jesus Christ, who consistently challenged the logic of violence by calling his followers to love their enemies and to respond to evil with kindness. In celebrating Christ's resurrection, Christians proclaim to the world that violence and death do not have the last word.

"True Christians," wrote Menno Simons, the early Anabaptist leader, "do not know vengeance. They are the children of peace. Their hearts overflow with peace. Their mouths speak peace, and they walk in the way of peace."

Sometimes this commitment to loving enemies has led Christians, following the pattern of Christ, to sacrifice their own lives as martyrs. More often, however, Christian compassion for others has found expression in far less dramatic forms: in quiet acts of kindness to a spouse or a stranger; in a gentle and patient attitude toward children; in a generosity of time and resources given to the poor, the sick, and the vulnerable; in a conscious commitment to speak the truth or to resist the impulse to gossip; in promoting the welfare of the local community; in finding points of connection with peoples and cultures beyond our own country. In these, and countless other ways, Christians seek to allow God's unconditional love for everyone to permeate their lives—to incarnate God's love into daily life so that the world might be transformed.

The invitation to become a Christian is an invitation to live in the power of love.

Living in the Gap: Healing and Hope

In summary, Christian faith offers a rich and compelling account of the human condition. With unflinching insight it describes our daily experience of living in that precarious space between hope and despair, between life and death, between the world as we know it should be and the world as we often experience it. Christian faith affirms that the yearnings deep within us for intimacy, beauty, harmony, and love are *true* voices—not merely cultural creations or the accident of our psychological makeup. Our desire for a life filled with meaning and purpose is an echo of something genuine, no less real than the evidence all around us that the world is fragmented and broken.

Christianity, however, goes beyond merely describing the

human condition. It also invites us into a living relationship with God, a God whose love for us fills our lives with meaning and joy. To be sure, the reality of God's love does not ultimately erase the gap that we experience between hope and despair. But it does invite us to live with purpose within the gap.

The invitation to faith is therefore an invitation to healing. To become a Christian is to participate in God's ongoing work of reconciliation: turning despair into joy, extending forgiveness to former enemies, transforming prejudices, finding freedom from the burdens of wealth and status, restoring dignity to those living in shame, extending compassion to those who have gone forgotten. In their daily lives, Christians bear witness to the possibility of healed minds, bodies, spirits, and relationships.

The invitation to faith is also an invitation to hope. For even as we participate in the healing work of God, we recognize that sin and selfishness have not disappeared from the world. We still live in bodies that get sick and will eventually die. We are still limited by the confines of our language and culture. The gap between what is and what ought to be remains. In biblical language, we still "see through a glass darkly." But followers of Christ live in a hope that keeps calling us back into the messiness of the fallen world. We choose to live *within the gap*, proclaiming to a doubting world that humans are not only physical but also spiritual beings. We proclaim that even though power corrupts, we can still dream of creating communities where power is redeemed. We proclaim that even as we confess our sinful inclinations, we still press on toward the goal of the kingdom of God.

The invitation to live in the gap is as clear today as it was two thousand years ago, when Jesus first encountered Peter and Andrew along the shores of Lake Galilee. And it is every bit as radical.

If you accept that invitation, you will be joining a great company of people who are on a journey. That journey will not always be easy, the path will not always be clear, and you may find yourself stumbling along the way. But the journey will be an adventure, and it will be a journey of joy. "Come," Jesus says, "drop what you are doing. Leave behind your old ways of thinking and acting. Come, and follow me."

The Author

John D. Roth is professor of history at Goshen College in Indiana, where he also serves as director of the Mennonite Historical Library and editor of *The Mennonite Quarterly Review*. He and his wife Ruth are the parents of four daughters and are active members in the Berkey Avenue Mennonite Fellowship. Roth is the editor of *Engaging Anabaptism: Conversations with a Radical Tradition* (2001) and the author of *Choosing Against War: A Christian View* (2002).